Building Wealth
Through Property

Hong Kong Expat Edition

"How to find, buy and revalue Hong Kong residential property for prosperity"

Michelle Cheng

Copyright © 2017 Michelle Cheng

All rights reserved.

ISBN-13: 978-1546571483

Table of Contents

	Acknowledgement	5
Chapter 1	Getting on the First Rung	7
Chapter 2	Collecting Your Little Green Ones	31
Chapter 3	The Buyer's Agent	50
Chapter 4	The Power of Leveraging	61
Chapter 5	The Rules of the Game	76
Chapter 6	I don't feel comfortable buying property in a different country.	78
Chapter 7	I want to buy a property to help my family out.	85
Chapter 8	Who's going to look after my property when I'm not there?	88
Chapter 9	Airbnb	92
Chapter 10	I want that holiday home I've dreamed about.	113
Chapter 11	How do I buy Hong Kong property?	120
Chapter 12	Is it a good time to buy property?	129
Chapter 13	I'll wait for another black swan event.	133
Chapter 14	The Secret to Your Success	145
Chapter 15	The Six Steps to Buying Property	159
Chapter 16	Looking Forward	184
	Where can you find Michelle Cheng?	187

Acknowledgment

I would like to express my gratitude to the many people who saw me through this book; to all those who provided support, talked things over, read, wrote, offered comments, allowed me to quote their ideas and opinions and assisted in the editing, proofreading and design.

I would like to thank Todd Pallett who was the driving force for enabling me to publish this book. Above all I want to thank my mother, Rosa Cheng and the rest of my family, who supported and encouraged me in throughout this process. It was a long and difficult journey and I'm grateful for their support.

I would like to thank Wallie Sohl and Alan Clark who were the key individuals who guided me through the muddy financial waters for the last ten years. I look forward to the next ten.

Thanks to Chris Liem at Engel & Voelkers who took time and was patient in gearing me up for this fast pace business.

Last and not least: I beg forgiveness of all those who have been with me over the course of the years and whose names I have failed to mention.

Chapter One:
Getting on the First Rung

A colleague who taught advanced mathematics at the last school I worked at once told me that the educational systems in many parts of the world do not prepare students well enough for the world.

School teaches students how to calculate the angles of a triangle, they teach them that a simile is a figure of speech involving the comparison of one thing to another with the help of the words "like" or "as", and that in August 1492, Columbus sailed the ocean blue. It is wonderful that students not only build their breadth of knowledge in all types of subjects but they are also given opportunities later to choose which fields they wish to pursue in depth for their tertiary education.

However, my colleague explains that even though schools cover various topics and subjects, they give students many different opportunities to try out new experience in life, there is one subject that rarely gets even an hour in any high school class. That topic is money management. There is no course in any school or any university that teaches students how to save, invest or grow their money. Well, maybe some business management teacher might graze lightly on how to balance your spread sheet but there's no concrete lesson on what you should do with your money in order to make it work for you.

This was very true for me. I came out of high school and university graduating with an Arts degree from the University of British Columbia and thinking to myself… what do I do now? I didn't have any skills, I didn't have any money and I had a small student loan accumulated that I needed to start paying off. I didn't really have a clue as to what I wanted to do with my life.

Any traditional Chinese father wanted his child to grow up to be a doctor, lawyer or even an accountant. Stereotypically, children of Asian descent were expected to either go into business or sciences and find a career that enabled them to support their entire extended family. Unfortunately for me, I didn't have a good guidance-counselling department at my school so I didn't know of all the possible avenues I could have taken with my life. I wasn't sure if I wanted to go into sciences and at that time in the 90s, getting into the university's business school was fiercely competitive.

I was just an average B+ student. I enjoyed school somewhat but I think at that age, I really didn't know what I wanted to do after I graduated from university. I practically bumbled my way through four years of university and finished still not knowing what I wanted to do in life. Tertiary education only gave you a diploma after you completed all their requirements. You learnt certain skills but were you able to apply them in life.

Looking Up From the Bottom of the Ladder

I graduated with an Arts degree double majoring in History and Asian Studies from the University of British Columbia. Great! Now what? What was I going to do with a degree like that? I did have some work experience. I worked as a teller at HSBC and as a customer service representative at a company now called Rogers Canada. For a few years of monotonous work, I answered the phone and listened to angry customers explaining that they had no idea how they were able to rack up a $20 a month plan to $300 of additional charges. I would get Chinese clients who would call up asking for assistance on how to change their settings on their phone but they can't make out the words on the screen because they can't read English! This wasn't something I wanted to do for the rest of my life so I decided to go back to school and possibly complete a teaching degree to become a teacher hoping that maybe this was something that I may enjoy doing more. All my life, I have been around teachers so that was basically the only profession I somewhat was familiar with.

Now you may ask, what does my book, "Building Wealth Through Property....Hong Kong Expat Edition" have to do with my beginnings in becoming a school teacher. Well, like I said, my life was not laid out before me in stone. I did not come from a wealthy Chinese family who provided me with a big trust fund. My parents come from humble beginnings.

My mother was in her early 20s when she relocated to Vancouver. She was hired on as a flight attendant by a Canadian airline and my father worked briefly for a diamond company in Hong Kong before getting on a plane to fly to Vancouver to be with my mother.

Getting on the First Rung

My mother only worked for the airline for a brief time before I came along so she found a job as a teller at a bank while my father applied to technical college at BCIT (British Columbia Institute of Technology). He studied to become an electrical technician and was hired by the city's hydroelectric company (BC Hydro). He worked there for almost forty years until he recently retired.

Later, my mother worked as an office administrator but quit about the time I graduated high school. After that, she decided to pursue one of her hobbies of interest, which she eventually turned, into a full-fledged non-profit business in Vancouver.

As early as I can remember, every time we drove somewhere around town, on the tape deck in that old white Nissan Datsun, my dad would have some Cantonese soprano blaring away on the speakers. My father enjoyed listening to Cantonese opera. Even now if you take a walk along the old streets of Sheung Wan or even along Temple Street in Yau Ma Tei, you will see some old grandfather sitting there in the park and he would have some Cantonese operetta singing away on his radio. This is truly an acquired taste for the old Chinese. The younger generation would consider this art form as something that belongs to the older generation. It is very much like thousand year old eggs. You either love it in the morning with your congee or you don't.

Cantonese opera is currently a dying art. For something to do as a couple, my parents enrolled themselves in Cantonese opera singing lessons in Richmond on the weekends. It was also a way they were able to socialize with other Chinese immigrants who had moved from Hong Kong.

Like most typical Chinese kids, I was made to learn some sort of musical instrument. Yes, it was the piano for me. But my mother decided that while she enrolled me in piano lessons, she enrolled herself in voice lessons. This was a bit atypical for parents. Since the kid was enrolled in piano lessons why don't I take singing lessons as well? She is a person who has always been a learner. The apple doesn't fall far from the tree because I developed the same traits as well.

When my parents finally decided to take Cantonese singing lessons together, my mother basically flew with it. Singing the role of the soprano in Cantonese opera is very much like Barry Gibb's falsetto in "Jive Talking." But with her European operatic voice training, she had the foundation and basically took to the art like a duck to water.

Talk about going to the extreme of turning a hobby into a career. She had such a strong interest that she started a small Cantonese singing troupe which she nurtured and eventually grew into a non-profit organization called the Vancouver Cantonese Opera. Now, her company annually produces full shows and various community works throughout the Vancouver Greater Lower Mainland.

She also gives lessons and does charity work for the Chinese community in order to promote this dying art form. For an immigrant to Canada, she has become a pretty strong and aggressive marketer of her talent and art form. She has turned a midlife crisis into a second career after the kids had all grown up and flew the coop!

Both my parents are hardworking individuals. My father always was the more cautious one with money. Being the patriarch of the family, he had to make sure that, my mom and his two kids, my little brother, Christopher, and myself were well provided for and had a roof over our heads. They both still made sure to give us all the opportunities we could possibly have. My mother is a decent young mother. She didn't pay too much attention to my schooling because she had a tougher job with my brother.

My parents didn't have much money. They left Hong Kong in their early 20s hoping to start a new life in Canada. The rules and requirements to immigrate to Canada in the 70s were very different to what they are now. My parents were just a young couple who wanted a new life and opportunity in Canada.

My family was quite frugal and did not spend extravagantly so I did learn quickly the value of a dollar. It wasn't until I moved to Hong Kong that I saw materialism and wealth to its full extent. In Vancouver, we only bought something if we needed it and when we bought it, we basically kept it until it died out or was on its last legs. You would never throw out an old pair of shoes.

My first car was a 1979 grey Volvo GL. My father bought that car new in 1979. He drove it for thirteen years and when I turned sixteen I drove the Volvo for another eleven years before I passed it down to my cousin, Desmond. That car was like a tank on wheels. The paint job was so old that by the time Desmond got the car, the paint was matte in colour because the shine from the paint was completely gone.

Now that's money well spent. Of course I would have liked to have a nice BMW or Mercedes like most of the Asian kids in Vancouver because that was their car of choice they would ask for from their satellite parents who were still working in Hong Kong.

My contribution to the student parking lot did not add the latest high-class edition that many other rich wealthy Chinese kids drove but that was out of my control. I wasn't in any financial position to afford a new car myself. So you can tell that my life growing up in Vancouver was fairly normal and non-privileged.

So I would not have imagined becoming a homeowner at twenty-five. But I did. I would have told you myself that you must have mistaken me for one of those rich Asian kids driving away in that latest Porsche their father bought them for their high school graduation gift. Most of my friends were not from privileged families either most were pretty down to earth.

My First Real Estate Friend

One of these friends whom I met early on in life is Wallie Sohl. I met him through a mutual friend who rented a room in Wallie's house. Wallie is a successful realtor for ReMax Canada whose main catchment area is Richmond, British Columbia. He and his business partners for years have followed the simple passive investment strategy of "buy and hold."

Wallie has many hobbies and interests. One hobby he got me into was motorcycle riding. He and his friends would go on road trips through the United States, along the coasts and deserts of the country. He also takes bike trips through Europe, Central America and Asia.

My parents dreaded my motorcycle riding and both my parents were pretty tight lipped when I rode home on my first Kawasaki Ninja 250 bike. That was my little commuter bike during my last years at university. It was Wallie who guided me well and gave me the right advice on how to get into motorcycle riding. "Take a course, learn how to ride the right way and then get a bike." After 13 years living in Hong Kong, I still enjoy the time on a motorcycle. Just last summer I drove down to Olympia, Washington and took the California Superbike two-day track course with the legendary Keith Code.

I would say that Wallie was instrumental for me owning my first home. Being a salesman and entrepreneur, he was also a great teacher of property. Every time I flew back to Vancouver to visit my family and friends, he and I would go for a car ride and he would drive me around town to see some of the new developments he would be working on.

I remember in the early 2000s the prices for property were not as high as they are now. He showed me brand new two and three bedroom condos in East Richmond, which were approximately three hundred to four hundred thousand, and townhouses were around five hundred thousand. With 20/20 hindsight, these units were a steal because now those units have almost doubled in price. Even at those prices, they were not something I could have afforded. However, it was still nice to dream of the possibly of owning something one day. Then it happened.

Grabbing opportunity when you see it.

One day, one of my uncles who was also a real estate agent told my mother that he was selling a small condo in Whalley for only $55,000.00. He told me that the unit was priced this low because it was a bank foreclosure and that the bank was selling the remainder of the loan. The unit and the entire building was a "leaky condo."

During this time, the Greater Vancouver area of British Columbia's Lower Mainland experienced a construction boom in the multi-family condominium market. This attracted developers, designers, contractors, workers, and new building technologies that contributed towards a booming housing industry.

However, many of these people came from climates that were quite different to the coastal region of B.C. (British Columbia) and did not understand what designs supported B.C.'s rainy climate. The major architectural designs of many of the condominiums that were built in the 1980s-1990s times were Postmodern, which featured building styles and forms reminiscent of the Mediterranean and southern California.

Unbeknownst to many of these individuals, Greater Vancouver receives over 161 rainy days per year and rainfall between 1153 and 2477 mm (45 to 97 inches) per year, approximately double that of London, England; triple that of Rome, Italy; and more than quadruple that of Los Angeles. With an average high summer temperature of 21-22 degrees Celsius, buildings dry out much less quickly (or not at all) compared to those in southern California or Mediterranean climates where average high summer temperatures of 28-30 degrees Celsius and above.

The older building designs in coastal B.C. provided greater protection from the damp and rainy climate than newer designs until this time, through the use of features such overhanging roofs, which protected the walls below from direct rain contact. The new Post Modernist designs that were more suitable for the hot and dry climates of warmer locations like California were not suitable for the wet and damp conditions of Vancouver.

The common building elements of this Post Modern design included roof parapet with no overhangs or eaves, stucco wall cladding, open walkways, arched windows, complex cladding joints, all of which provided more opportunities for penetration of water which contributed to leakage, deterioration, rot and mould due to precipitation.

During this time, this ordeal in Vancouver was known as the "leaky condo crisis." The majority of the buildings that experienced these problems were owned by the individual owners of condominium units. Many homeowners were faced with needing to correct a problem they did not create, by a contractor they had not hired; they purchased the units either from a previous owner, a developer, or a developer/contractor.

Typical repair costs were in the tens or even hundreds of thousands of dollars, resulting in significant hardship, bankruptcies, and lawsuits against the developers, contractors, architects, and others involved in the original construction and maintenance of the buildings. Many first-time homeowners could do nothing more but walk away from their homes and the banks foreclosed on them.

So back to this original unit…

When you are looking at property, you really need a good real estate agent you trusted who can give clear-cut advice.

Was this unit a good buy? The price was amazing and it was even cheaper than buying a new car at the time but I wasn't familiar with the process of acquiring a foreclosed unit. My uncle wasn't too much help either.

So I called Wallie to see if he had any experience in this matter. Wallie has been in the real estate business for many years both in acquiring and selling property of his own too. He also worked closely with many big developers in and around the city. While most estate agents focus only on moving volume and closing sales for their clients, Wallie worked also in building his own wealth through property.

When Wallie takes you around to a new development he is a well knowledged salesman. He can tell you a lot about the development - how the building was constructed, what building materials were used and what issues have been overcome by city council and what approvals are currently underway.

He believes not only in looking at the end result of selling a property to a client, he sees that the location, city planning and gentrification improvements are all factors you need to consider when determining whether an area has the potential for capital growth. This is something I will discuss more in the later chapters.

Wallie is very involved in understanding and is continuously learning about many aspects of property from land approvals, construction, management, maintenance and property law. This is something I aspire to because being a teacher. I believe that having a stronger understanding of the business strengthens your position in the market.

As for the "leaky condo crisis", many people in the city were well aware of this issue. You would hear it on the evening news about on-going legal battles and resolutions homeowners had to face to repair their homes and move on from this ordeal.

When I told Wallie I was interested in purchasing this $55,000.00 unit but wasn't too sure of the process, Wallie asked me three questions that every person should consider when looking at purchasing property.

Question #1: Is the location of the unit ideal for a tenant or for you to live?

This question can be inclusive or exclusive of each other. Do not always buy a place based on whether you will live in it. Because your preferences can be different to someone else's, where you may not like to live, someone else may for different reasons. Many investors I have spoken with have expressed their regrets for not buying when they were given the opportunity because they didn't buy because they would not personally have wanted to live there. In the end, they regretted not purchasing the place.

Many did not go through with the purchase because they felt it was a place they would not want to live in but later realize that a few years down the road, the location they were looking in became a highly desired area of town with little turnover and high yield.

In this scenario, I was buying for personal use. The unit was in Whalley, Central Surrey. At that time, Whalley was still considered a more rough part of Surrey. It was about a forty minutes drive from Vancouver and more than an hour during rush hour. The skytrain extended into that area of Surrey and with the easier access of transportation, it attracted vagrants and juveniles looking for trouble.

The city of Surrey has hopes to gentrify this area by encouraging more middle-income families to move there. By building more affordable housing closer to the train stations, it wanted to encourage people to move further out to Surrey and commute into Vancouver by train.

For the majority of the population of Vancouver, most people drive. The average household owns from 2 to 3 vehicles so most people commute to work by car because the public transit system was very limited in its reach. The demand to live by a train station was not high ten years ago though I believe that demand has risen now after the 2010 Winter Olympics, the city has extended more lines to reach further out into the suburbs.

Now for a person living in Hong Kong, the demand to live by a train station is extremely high because most of the population do not own cars or on many occasions, travelling by subway is cheaper, more affordable and convenient.

Areas like the Peak or in the Pokfulam areas on Hong Kong Island where there is no subway access, it is a lifestyle choice that people choose to live there because they can afford their own transportation or are willing to sacrifice the journey for cheaper rent or cheaper housing prices.

Areas like Kennedy Town, Sai Ying Pun and now Wong Chuk Hang where the MTR stations now reach, those locations are now more desirable leading to increases in property prices.

Wallie's question is key to all questions regarding real estate. Location, location, and location! Is this where you want to buy? The answer was no. I didn't really like that area and the thought of moving out of my parents' place that was in a nicer part of Surrey to a rougher area STILL in Surrey even though there was the convenience of the train station still did not appeal to me. The location was not ideal.

Question #2: Have you checked with the strata management regarding any rules or conditions for living in the building?

Usually if you are the first owner of the condominium, you are grandfathered or exempted from many of the conditions of living in the unit including pet ownership. However, after the establishment of the strata council in the building, if conditions such as restrictions on pet ownership have been established, these rules need to be followed. In this particular building the strata council did not allow pets for tenants and owners.

For some property owners who don't have pets, this would be a nonissue. They wouldn't see animals ruining the gardens and landlords wouldn't have to worry if the animal would ruin the interior of their homes. But for pet owners who are looking to rent or buy in these buildings this rule would greatly deter them from considering.

Toby, my dog, lived for sixteen years before he passed. He was part of the family so buying a place that he wasn't allowed to visit or come by was not a place I would consider buying. Having rules like not allowing pets into the building kill the life of the building because it limits the type of renters and owners who would rent or live in the building.

Question #3: Why would you want to buy into a building that you clearly know had structural flaws?

The strata management had already spent thousands of dollars paying for all the repairs to eliminate the leaking problems in the building so if I were to buy a unit in the building now, I would not be responsible in contributing to the cost. However, who is to tell me that there might not be any further issues that may arise because of the past leakage issues?

Mould and fungus often grow in leaky Metro Vancouver buildings. When repairs are carried out for leaky condos, major structural changes and repairs are often required which usually involve mould remediation to some degree. If the remediation of the mould is not thorough, elevated levels of mould may remain within the building even after remediation.

Often, after leaky condo restoration work is complete, proper mould clearance testing is not done to verify safe levels of mould within the individual condo unit living areas. So prolonged exposure to damp and mouldy environments may cause a variety of health effects, or none at all. Some people are sensitive to moulds. For these people, moulds can cause nasal stuffiness, throat irritation, coughing or wheezing, eye irritation, or, in some cases, skin irritation.

If I already know of issues that have occurred in a building, what is the chance that there will be more problems in the future? Is this a risk I am willing to take? Do I even need to take such a risk? Buying your first home for many is usually the largest purchase some people would make. Unfortunately for the previous homeowner who walked away from this unit leaving it to foreclose, I'm not sure whether it is a good idea for me to walk right into the mess again.

A Trusted Real Estate Agent

Wallie's conclusion on the unit was clear: even though the price was good, I still should not consider moving forward with the purchase because of the potential risks. He instead suggested another unit he knew of. A great point here is to build a good relationship with a trusted estate agent.

(For questions you should ask when considering picking a real estate agent, go to my website and check out http://michelle-cheng.com)

Wallie knew of another unit that was under foreclosure and the court date was actually in two weeks time. The unit was in Richmond near the city center. The building was a low-rise three-floor building that was built in the early 70s so the exterior material of the building and the roof overhang was made from cedar and not the more recent stucco that was not withstanding the wet conditions of the Lower Mainland. The building was in a low-density area and it was walking distance to many restaurants, shopping malls and located right behind one of the local community colleges.

The building allowed animals and the reason why the apartment was in foreclosure was that the owner was unable to continue paying the mortgage. The condition of the building was good. Wallie was going to buy it himself but he offered it to me if I wanted to go for it. I made the decision to proceed so we showed up on the auction day at the courthouse.

Buying a foreclosure unit.
Going to an auction, you think that it may be a well-attended event but on that day, it was quiet. Some people who know about this secret would squat often at the courthouses hoping to pick up deals. Actually during this time of the condo crisis, many apartment units and town houses were being foreclosed on so if you had cash and time to sit at the courthouses, you would walk home having picked up cheap property.

The lender (bank) would specify the "reserve price" which was the minimum they will accept to transfer the property. The unit was listed for $69,000.00. The procedure for bidding on the property was a silent one-time bid.

The bids were written down, the bailiff took the bids and presented them to the judge. The judge looked at the two bids and commented that there was just a $500 difference between bids. He declared that the property would go to me stating that I made the higher bid. On that day I purchased a 500 square foot one bedroom unit property for $72,000.00 Canadian dollars (USD$53,700.00/£44,004.00). I made it onto the first rung of the ladder.

Chapter Two:
Collecting Your Little Green Ones

The hardest thing to do in regards to property purchasing is to get on the first rung of the ladder. Especially when you are just starting out in life, some of you may have some educational debt that you have accumulated and you are just beginning to put some money away for a rainy day. How are you going to do it?

In Canada, banks do offer good lending packages for first homebuyers. At that time from my recollection, Canadian banks allowed first time homebuyers to put as little as 5% down towards their down payments.

As a first homebuyer, I still needed my agent to guide me through these unknown waters. He had a mortgage broker who quickly found a bank who offered me a mortgage at a good interest rate. I didn't need to walk into any bank until the paperwork was all done and all I needed to do was to sign the final papers. Wallie had a great solicitor who he still works with today who pushed all the paperwork painlessly through. The entire process ran exceptionally smooth especially since everything was dealt with mostly over the phone.

I had some savings put away and had an insurance claim that I cashed in to have $15,000.00 towards the down payment. If I only put down 5% of the sales price, by the time I sold the property, my cash on cash return would have been very nice. But I decided to put in more so that my mortgage amount was only $57,000.00 and at such low interest rates my monthly payments was around $350.00. This was cheaper than the going rental rates in that area too. After I completed on the unit, I moderately fixed the place up, changed the carpet to basic laminate flooring, added a new coat of paint, retiled the bathroom, I moved in. I was a homeowner.

Moving to Hong Kong

However, a year and a half later, I completed all my teaching certification at the university and was offered a teaching position in Tin Shui Wai, Hong Kong. I packed up my things, gave some furniture away, moved my things back to my mom's house, found a tenant for my unit and flew to Hong Kong. After

Collecting Your Little Green Ones

I completed one year of teaching, I flew back and decided to put the unit on the market and look for a buyer. This time, I asked for $180,000.00 but accepted an offer for $175,000.00.

Of course Wallie was the agent who sold it for me. So just in a matter of a few years, the compound annual growth on that unit was 34.45%. From an investment of $15,000.00 minus the loan from the bank I made a profit of $118,000.00. That's about $40,000.00 growth each year, which beats any type of mutual fund!

Again, property purchasing works very well if you know the right people you trust. My story will move a bit quicker now that I was working in Hong Kong. During my second year teaching, my mother gave me a call from Vancouver one evening. She was having dim sum with a friend who was considering on selling one of her units in Hong Kong. My mother asked her if she would consider selling it to me. Now, just to give you a bit of background, my geographical knowledge of Hong Kong was still very limited. In my first year, I was posted to Tin Shui Wai, New Territories and in my second year, I taught and lived at St. Stephen's Primary School in Stanley by St. Stephen's beach. My housing was all provided for in my first two years of teaching in Hong Kong so I knew very little about the rental market of Hong Kong.

My mother told me that her friend was selling one of her units on Caine Road in the Mid Levels. You'd laugh but I had no idea where that was or how lucrative owning a place in Central was. My mother knew because she and my dad grew up in that area when they were kids. So she told me to meet up with her friend's daughter to see the place.

So I did. Still oblivious to what I was looking at, I met up with the lady, and she took me to the unit. It was a tiny flat to my uneducated eyes. In Canada, kids grow up in houses that are from 1000 to 2500 square foot in size. Our home in Surrey was 2500 square feet with a surrounding back and front yard for my dog to run in.

In this unit on Caine road, I was standing in what was said to be on paper a 400 square foot apartment with a two-bedroom layout. It was in its original floor plan with that old dark teak wood flooring that a lot of expats don't like.

"So how was it? Is it any good?" my mom asked the next day. "Yeah sure," I said, "let's go for it." Inside I had no idea whether this was a good buy or not but I knew that land ownership is always the way to go. There wasn't anything wrong with the unit structurally, it had a great view, and the vendor was motivated to sell. If you see opportunity, you should seize it, shouldn't you?

So we found a solicitor to draw up the paperwork, I used the proceeds from the sale of my property in Richmond towards the down payment on my next property. In the spring of 2006, I paid HKD$2,230,000.00 which was the market asking price for a two bedroom, 400 square foot apartment on Caine Road in the Mid Levels of Hong Kong.

It wasn't the prettiest unit by far. It was in its original layout and original furnishings. The floor had the dark teak wood flooring and the kitchen and bathroom were pretty dated. Even in this condition, the bank valuation price still listed it at $2.23 million. In Hong Kong, the banks basically control the property market by setting out valuation prices for all properties. Whether the unit was newly renovated or in dire condition, banks will still value it the same when it comes to the building and its address. They look at recent sales and any other factors that could contribute to the value of the property.

That's why when I have clients now who come to me to say that they don't mind purchasing old, dilapidated units because they plan to spend more money to do renovations, I remind them to not over capitalise on their investment because the money they put into the renovation does not increase the value of the property in Hong Kong.

This is a unique issue for property in Hong Kong. In other countries, if you decide to add an extension to your property or dig a basement below your house, you actually add value to your property. In Hong Kong, however, unapproved extensions are considered illegal and the government will require you to bring the place back to its original plan. Banks will not value newly renovated flats any more than units that are still in their original dated conditions. They simply look at the address and recent transactions sold in the building to valuate your property.

If you need to renovate, moderate your costs and keep in mind that renovations will only increase your happiness of living there, if you plan to live there or increase the likelihood and ability for you to rent out the unit to potential tenants.

It is difficult to get into the Hong Kong property market. Even during the early 2000s, buying an apartment that was only 400 square feet costed over $300,000.00 Canadian dollars. This was still an enormous about of money for some. It came up to $819.00 Canadian dollars ($5575 Hong Kong dollars) per square foot. Little did we all know, the price per square foot has almost tripled in the last ten years.

I could have purchased a much nicer place in Vancouver but I was in Hong Kong and little did I know then, I was here to stay much longer. I was very fortunate to have bought around that time because looking at the Hong Kong house price index I bought in practically at the lowest point because from that point on the market started to climb. Now 10 years later, and even after the 2008 Financial Crisis this small piece of property that I thought was extremely expensive to buy has now almost tripled in value. Looking back at it now, I'm amazed how well it has done.

	Golden Pavilion, 66 Caine Road, Mid Levels			
	Purchased	March 2005	2017 HSBC Bank Valuation	$6.38M
	Price	$2.38M	Estimated Rent	$20K per month
	Saleable Area (sf)	315	Age of Building	22 years
	Total Growth/Per Annum Compound	151% Total 8.75% pa	Gross Yield on Initial Purchase	10% per annum

(NOTE: You can see more about how I started my property investment with my webinar with Todd Pallet, at http://michelle-cheng.com)

The Ball is Rolling

Here is where all the fun starts. With the help of the market, after a few years, slowly my Caine road unit began to rise in value. The bank started to value the unit more than what I originally paid for so when I approached the bank after three years and asked to borrow against the equity my original down payment went from 40% down to 20% of the Loan-to-Value ratio so now I was able to borrow back up to 60% of the total value of the property.

From that equity I used the money to purchase other units and repeated the process elsewhere. Keep in mind that it wasn't just the money I pulled from this one unit that enabled me to finance all my other purchases. I did put a lot of work into gathering my funds. For many years, I budgeted my salary fiercely and I also opened revolving line of credits with banks to bridge the money when it came time to completing these purchases.

I wasn't an extravagant spender either. It would have been nice to have the latest handbag or shoes but that didn't really interest me. Even now when I tell myself that after a sale of one of my properties I will go out and treat myself a new pair of shoes I end up not getting anything because I don't really need them. I was already looking ahead at my next investment purchase.

Buying my first off-plan purchase.

The second unit I bought was actually with my mother when she was visiting from Vancouver, and this was completely on a whim. There was no preplanning, no talk prior between us on buying a second apartment together in Hong Kong. Although I believe my mother had thoughts about this for a while. This was something completely impulsive and actually many Hong Kong people do when they buy property because the market pace is extremely fast. Who can pass up a good deal when they see one? One property can only have one buyer so if you miss the opportunity it is gone forever. I remember the day quite vividly.

I was in my third teaching year now. It was mid August and I was at my new school just preparing some material for the start of the year. I was leaving school for the day and plan to meet my mother for dinner somewhere in Yau Mai Tei, Kowloon. I had brought some books to school so I was dragging along a small carry-on suitcase. When I met up with her, she told me that she wanted to do some apartment window-shopping…. just before we go to dinner.

We walked into one of the local agencies just off the street. There are over forty thousand agents in Hong Kong so imagine how would one real estate agent stand out from the rest? The agent was a local Chinese man. He was young, probably in his early 20s. He was smartly dressed but he was a bit over the top with all the high-end name brands to a point that I felt a bit underdressed.

Now that I'm in the same business, I have noticed that on some occasions you do need to mirror your clientel. In our case that day, in my Birkenstock sandals, jean skirt and Gap T-shirt dragging my no-name suitcase, that I bought at the Lo Wu shopping centre in Shenzhen, I wasn't quite mirroring back!

He took us around the area to look at two units but my mom wasn't too impressed. Then like any good salesman, he did some probing and asked if we'd be interested in seeing the fifth and last phase of a new off-plan site called Park Island being launched that evening.

Now again, this was still my third year in Hong Kong. By this time, I had moved into the unit on Caine Road but was just starting to familiarize myself with the geography around

Hong Kong. I lived in Tin Shui Wai, in the New Territories and the second year I lived in Stanley. At that time, Stanley was not as big of a tourist spot as it is today. The boardwalk that is there now was not yet built so it still felt like a quiet village on the south side of Hong Kong island.

Park Island is located in Ma Wan next to the Tsing Ma Bridge. When you head towards or when you come back from the Chek Lap Kok Airport, you see Park Island off to the side from the bridge. It is a tiny island with thirty-one tall apartment blocks that stretch from one end to the other of the island. It is very much like a resort with outdoor and indoor pools, resort facilities, restaurant and bars. It is not as busy as the more westernized part of Discovery Bay but I believe that with a little more time, it will get busier.

Like Discovery Bay, the island does not permit personal vehicles to enter so it is only accessible by taxi, a ferry from Central and by public transit bus from the airport, Tsing Yi and Tsuen Wan MTR stations. It is a car free zone that only allows trucks and moving vans access during business hours so the island remains quiet and serene. The location sounded appealing so we decided to go with the agent to see the launch that evening.

I guess you can say we were two golden geese that unknowingly walked into this agent's shop on the right day at the right time. He made sure he did not leave our side for the entire event.

Back to the development launch of Park Island, the experience felt very much like cattle coming to auction. When we arrived, we were corralled through the sales area and into the show room. The showroom wasn't extremely helpful in showing us what a standard unit would look like. The rooms were brightly lit with flood lights, the choice of furniture was not to my taste and the walls were made of clear one inch thick Plexiglas so basically you had no way of gauging a true sense of the size of the units so overall it was difficult to know what you were looking at.

Stress, stress, stress

When you buy off plan properties, it literally means you are buying from a plan. Sometimes, the developer may not even have laid any foundation work on the construction site so all you

Collecting Your Little Green Ones

are basing your purchase decision from are the floor plans, the sketches and information packages provided by the developer. If you are not used to looking at property, this method of choosing a home may be daunting. Could you imagine spending a few million Hong Kong dollars on something you haven't seen?

Tower 31, Park Island, Ma Wan, New Territories				
	Purchased	April 2006	2017 HSBC Bank Valuation	$7.62
	Price	$3.22M	Estimated Rent	$22K per month
	Saleable Area (sf)	630	Age of Building	10 years
	Total Growth/ Per Annum Compound	109% Total 7.63% pa	Gross Yield on Initial Purchase	8% per annum
Brief: Long term investment property, 3-bedroom conversion to 2 bedrooms with office space and 1 bathroom. **Property:** Leasehold – Bus services to the airport, Tsing Yi and Kwai Fong. Ferry service access to and from Central. Convenient access to Disneyland. Renters of this unit usually are family and relatives of residents of Park Island.				

In the showroom, they had a miniature model of the site and they highlighted the last phase they were selling that evening. The most you could do was hold a copy of the floor plans look at the miniature and gauge which direction the unit would probably be facing. All the units had different square footage, different layouts, and various numbers of bedrooms, balcony or no balcony, ensuite or no ensuite. Given the fact that we just landed with this opportunity that day, we did not have much time to ponder and had to decide right on the spot if we wanted in on the purchase.

For these kinds of development launches in Hong Kong, you are given the choice to choose which unit you want to buy but you aren't given the choice of which floor. If everyone was given a choice, they would choose the highest floors; however, that choice is determined by ballot only. Basically one of the head agents would go into the drawing room and they would take turns and draw out a unit. We were hoping for a "B" unit so when they drew out a "B" ticket they would come to you and say, "We've drawn a B unit on the 30th floor, do you want it?"

What do we say? If we say no, the ballot would go to the next buyer and they will take the unit and the next ballot that will be drawn could be a unit on a lower floor. If we say yes to the first ballot, then we have just purchased a unit on Park Island and we will need to present the deposit right then and there. Once again, for some people, buying your first home is one of the biggest purchases in your life.

Buying a house at one of these Hong Kong events felt like looking at puppies from a window – do you want the little brown one with the floppy ears or the white one with the spots? You aren't allowed to touch the puppies and you had to decide which one you wanted to take home or someone else will. At the end of the day, we said yes and bought an 800 square foot unit costing $3,800,000.00 Hong Kong dollars. It was a fast decision buying something that large but it was only one of many experience for myself. By the end of the day, we went going home without any dinner.

Benefits to buying off-plan property

There are many benefits to buying off plan property because they can offer real advantages for first homebuyers. First homebuyers are generally short on cash and as a result have difficulty in finding funds quickly that are required for a finished property with a short-term settlement. In Hong Kong, the usual completion period of a second hand property purchase is between 6 to 8 weeks. Within that time period, you need to get the loan approval, solicitors underway and the deposit ready. In comparison to other countries, leaders for secondary home purchases in Hong Kong generally are less flexible in regards to the loan-to-value ratios than if you were buying in countries like Canada, USA, Australia or the UK.

Provisional purchase agreements on secondary properties in Hong Kong do not have "subject to" clauses so there is less flexibility on the stipulation and conditions of the sale. For example, if you are about to sign for a purchase of a property, there is no condition you can state that if you are not able to get financing for the sale, you are allowed to withdraw.

If you agree to a sale and the vendor has already accepted your initial deposit to the sale, if by any chance you need to withdraw from the sale, you lose your deposit and in addition could face additional suits files by the other party. An initial deposit can be between three to five percent of the sale price so that amount can be significant and a few weeks at the signing of the formal agreement, you are required to pay the second deposit of a similar amount.

Though buying off plans in Hong Kong still does not give you any 'subject-to" clauses that allow you to withdraw your intention to buy, it can give the homebuyer time – time to save for settlement, time to plan for settlement, potentially time for capital growth prior to settlement (as most developers offer lower prices and financial incentives at the start and put prices up once construction has commenced) and time to make all the relevant applications for any homeowner's grant.

Buying off plan will also give a homebuyer advantages not available to a purchaser of second hand property, such as:

- Stamp duty savings in many instances. Some developers will offer discounts as incentives for buyers.
- The ability to customise floor plans and finishes. Some developers offer a few choices of kitchen cabinetry and flooring.
- Most choice in terms of apartment types, which means greater choice of layouts, views and finishes. In our example, we were given a choice of which unit we wanted in the Park Island launch. Even though it was only from a floor plan, we were given the choice.
- Easy payment terms with only 10% deposit required and the balance due on settlement. This part may vary depending on the development.
- Often, interest on deposits can be received when cash deposits are paid.
- Security for deposits as all deposits are held in trust.

- Alternative deposits. Developers often give a few choices on how to pay the balance, offering various types of bonus or incentives.

My story segues more into off-plan properties but before you rush out and buy, know that there are many international property agencies that will ask you to come to their evening seminars where they will wine and dine you in order for you to hear about their latest property development in countries like the United Kingdom, United States and Australia.

If you're looking at foreign property, do your research, know your facts:

- Understand the median apartment prices growth, vacancy rates, rents, employment statistics and demographic. Get to know the area, transportation linkages, and current and planned infrastructure projects.
- Research the development team, who's going to deliver this project. What's the track record for the builder, developer, architect and sales agent? Can you go and visit some of the builder and developers recent projects?

- Get proper independent legal advice from a specialist property lawyer before signing anything.
- Understand the time frames around the delivery of the project and the sunset dates in the contract of sale.

Obviously there are some difficulties doing this on your own. By this time, I was in my sixth teaching year at Chinese International School so with a full time career, and also tutoring in the evening, how on earth was I able to educate myself on all these tips I've just told you?

Since then much has changed in Hong Kong with respect to off plan, first buy property. Is it as lucrative as it was ten years ago? I'm not so sure anymore but everyone has their own opinion but I am happy to chat it over with you over a cup of coffee one day.

Chapter Three:
The Buyer's Agent

Meet my buyer's agent, Alan Clarke. A buyer' agent exclusively represents you and your interests when looking at a property. They work side by side from the moment you begin your search to the day you get the keys to your new home.

They take the time to learn about you, analyse your needs in a home or investment property, and make recommendations based on that information. A buyer's agent is an expert on the local market and can advise you on neighbourhoods, trends and values. They can help you understand what you are able to afford, what kinds of homes suit your needs, and what might be the best value for you now and in the long run.

I met Alan Clarke when he was an advisor for a wealth management firm in Hong Kong. He lived here for close to 20 years before moving back to the UK to focus on the UK market. I've known Alan for a number of years and I can say that his road to riches required just as much hard work in building his success as a property owner and expert in the field.

Alan wasn't always in wealth management from the beginning. Believe it or not, Alan was a bobby in London. He entered the police force at the age of eighteen and a week later a financial officer from the bank came in to the police station and helped him set up a savings plan. At 21, he was approved for his first mortgage for a small three-bedroom house in Birmingham, which he and his dad renovated and turned into a four-bedroom property for student housing.

Throughout his career, Alan kept up his hobby of buying property around London, cleaning them up and renting them off. Just like myself, Alan had a stable profession that banks had confidence in and when it was time for him to leave the police force after thirteen years, he moved to Hong Kong to work in wealth management.

When I met Alan, I was looking for someone to help me manage my investment portfolio. Since I was in my teens, my mother helped me start an account holding various types of mutual funds. Basically the money I contributed was money I had saved from Chinese New Year and summers work wages I put away. Now that I've moved to Hong Kong, I thought that I should start a new investment savings plan to diversify my investments.

When I met Alan, he suggested purchasing foreign property as a means of investment. Before then I had not considered buying property strictly for investment. The three properties I have purchased up until then have all been for personal use. I lived in the apartment in Richmond, BC, I lived in the apartment on Caine Road and my family stays on Park Island whenever they visit Hong Kong. This was the first time someone suggested that I buy property for the sole purpose of investment.

Brick, glass and steel

Brick, glass and steel were the components of property investment. It is something you can see and touch. Alan told me in our first serious conversation on this topic that unlike stocks and bonds that you buy from the bank, when you invest in property, you are purchasing tangible assets – something that physically exists.

Of course there are downsides to this kind of investment. Once you have purchased your property, your money is not easily assessable. If you invested in stocks or bonds, you can pull your money out just by a click of a button. But how quickly can investment rise or fall? It is a commonly accepted truth on Wall Street that stocks fall 3 times faster than they rise. Many stocks during the 2008 Global Financial Crisis lost over 50% of their value in a matter of days.

The typical explanation borrows heavily from psychology and assumes fear of loss is greater than desire for gain. Investors will flee en masse when their profits are at risk, but are more timid when it comes to buying into a market so during the crisis, when stocks started to plummet, more and more investors pulled their money out of the stock market which hastened the speed of devaluation.

With property, even as the equity may devalue, it is more difficult to pull your money out because you need to find a buyer who would be motivated enough to buy in a down turning market. Without knowing where the bottom is, it would be rare that a buyer would be so willing to get into that market. Naturally the only thing that most property owners would do is to hold on to their property and hope that you'll come out the other side unscathed.

During the period of the 2008 Global Financial Crisis, I watched very closely while the value of my existing properties dropped those few months but since I had no reason to sell all I did was hold and in a matter of a few months, the bank valuations went back to their original values and started to increase again. I do believe that property is the great tangible asset to invest in that holds its value well in whatever upswing or downswing the markets are riding.

I am sure some highflying stockbroker will tell you that they invested in some amazing blue chip stock and made millions in a matter of days. Of course, that is one method of investing but as a teacher, I did not have the time nor knowledge to risk my money to catch the daily market upswings and downswings. I needed to be able to invest in something that moved in a less volatile pattern but still produce strong results so property was the one option I could manage to invest in during my off hours.

People who helped me along the way

I hope that by now you have realized that my journey has not been entirely all on my own, I had help every step of the way. My mother is a strong and very influential woman in my life who I can reluctantly admit now at the age of forty, has offered strong encouragement for my gutsy investment decisions. Wallie who is like a big brother to me, took me under his wing. He not only encouraged me to take up motorcycle riding (something that my parents weren't too happy with), he was instrumental in getting me on the first rung of that property investment ladder. Alan, the third person who helped me along, put me on the right investment path. Luckily he found me before I made any investment mistakes that could have been detrimental to my process.

Making those right choices

Some of you may know someone who has made those investment mistakes. Either they picked the wrong stock, got the wrong advice from an advisor or purchased a property that is now a money pit. This is what we all fear. With Alan, I basically struck gold in that sense. He is an honest man and someone I could trust who found me just at the right point in my life when I was ready to invest when my borrowing power was strong.

In Hong Kong, there are over forty thousand licensed real estate agents peddling their services at anyone off the street. Besides real estate agents there are insurance brokers, wealth management advisors and many other types of investment brokers asking you to invest with them. Who can you trust in helping you decide your future? How should you invest your hard earned cash?

I'm sure we all have met individuals who have approached you asking you to join some crazy investment scheme. There are so many that I've never heard about until I was approached. I have been offered to invest in modern Chinese art that would be circulated and rented out to commercial buildings.

I've been asked to invest in African trees that would be harvested into expensive tree oil or some crazy loon would tell me about this pyramid scheme wishing you were travelling around the world with them. We've all been approached by so many of these kinds of ideas or programs that promise to pay up to 30% annually. What they don't tell you is that it pays only to be at the top end of the tier.

With Alan, his proof, knowledge and experience is definitely in his pudding. Like myself, Alan started quite early building his financial portfolio. By the time I met Alan, he not only a massed a very strong portfolio in London property, he also accumulated a very healthy collection of properties in Hong Kong.

Now in the following chapters I'll break down more of what questions I had that helped me decide to go ahead with property purchasing in the UK but right now, I'll just quickly summarize.

With Alan's advice and assistance, I purchased and completed in the spring of 2010 on a one-bedroom unit for £217,500.00 near Bow station. Two years later in the winter of 2012, I completed on a small studio for £265,000.00 in Islington.

Both Wallie and Alan's philosophy in real estate investment was simple – **buy and hold**. They don't believe in flipping property. They believed in buying and holding to allow capital to grow. The locations that Alan found for me had good potential for gentrification or there were strong factors that predicted high growth in the coming years.

I did hold on to them for a few years but I sold the first one four years later (Q3 2014) and the second one two years after that (Q1 2016). I gained very well on the capital growth from both units, which enabled me to lay larger deposits on two other units. This time one was in West London and the second one was in the south. Both units cost around £400,000.00. So in a matter of five years, I doubled my investments.

Alan and I talk about property investing like it is the game of Monopoly©. You roll the dice, you pick up your game piece (Mine would always be the 40s-era Midget Race car) and you move around the board. When you land on a plot of land that is for sale, if you had money, you would buy the plot.

You continue around the board and if you land back on your plot of land you can build a little green house. If someone lands on your property, you can collect rent from the "tenant". You continue the process - building more little green houses, collecting rent - until you have enough green ones to trade in for a big red house.

You quickly realize that the more plots of land you own and the more little green houses you have built, the more rent you end up collecting.

Time and time again, I have had to persuade my friends that for their first property purchase they should not buy that big red one. Of course we all want that dream home when we get to a certain age but then we will trap ourselves in leveraging too much too soon.

Having to support your property investment strictly on active income (income that you need to work for) is too dangerous on the off chance that something may happen to you - you lose your job or you become too sick to work – you won't have that income stream to keep your finances afloat and once your savings run out your finances start crumbling.

Of course we all want that dream home sooner than later but don't throw all the money you have into one purchase. You need to start with something small. Buy smaller units first, hold them for a while and then when they have risen in value, put them on the market to sell. Only after repeating this process a few times will you have capital to buy that big red house without needing to borrow a large amount from the bank? Yes, some of you don't want to wait for that big day but invest smarter, not harder.

One thing I need to emphasize is that even though by this time I was doing quite well as an international schoolteacher and was earning a very respectable salary, I still could not have done this all strictly from the salary I was earning.

Chapter Four:
The Power of Leveraging

A science teacher would define a lever as a bar resting on a certain point that multiplies the force you exert making it easier to move or lift objects using less force. An economics teacher would define leverage as the act of using various financial instruments or borrowed capital in order to increase the potential return an investment.

"Leverage is the reason some people become rich and others do not." - Robert Kiyosaki

There is one thing that both the rich and the poor have equal amounts of. That is time. We all have 24 hours in a day, and how much money you make (and save) in that daily 24 hour cycle will determine how early you will be able to reach your financial goals.

Leveraging is a very powerful tool when used wisely. It allows you to create wealth and income using someone else's money. Consider the common real estate purchase requirement of a 20% down payment – or $100,000 on a $500,000 asset. The buyer is essentially using a relatively small percentage of his or her own money to make the purchase, and a lender is providing the majority of the money. Real estate investors often refer to the remainder of the purchase price as "other people's money," since persons other than the borrower provided the money needed to make the purchase.

Assuming the property appreciates at 5% per year, the borrower's net worth from this purchase would grow to $525,000 in just 12 months. Comparing this gain to the gain from an unleveraged purchase highlights that value of leverage. For example, the same borrower could have used the $100,000 to make an outright, paid-in-full purchase of a $100,000 property.

Assuming the same 5% rate of appreciation, the buyer's net worth from the purchase would have increased $5,000 over the course of 12 months versus $25,000 for the more expensive property. The $20,000 difference demonstrates the potential net worth increase provided through the employment of leverage.

Now, picture that 5% gain every year for 20 years. Over time, the use of leverage can have a significant, positive impact on your net worth.

The Dangers of Leverage

Just as leverage can work on your behalf, it can also work against you. Revisiting our earlier example, if you use a $100,000 down payment to purchase a $500,000 home, and real estate prices in your area decline for several years in a row, the leverage works in reverse. After year one, your $500,000 property could be worth $475,000 if it depreciates by 5%. A year after that, it could be worth $451,250 - a loss in equity of $48,750.

Under that same 5% price-decline scenario, if that $100,000 had been used for an all-cash purchase of a $100,000 home, the buyer would have lost just $5,000 the first year home prices fell.

In real estate markets where prices fall significantly, homeowners can end up owing more money on the house than the house is actually worth. For investors, declining prices can reduce or even eliminate profits. If rents fall too, the result can be a property that cannot be rented at a price that will cover the cost of the mortgage and other expenses.

The problems get even bigger when multiple units are involved, as real estate investors often put down as little money as possible. The goal is to leverage your money by taking control of 100% of the assets while only putting down 20% of the value. Consider the $500,000 we reviewed in our previous example.

Since the home is purchased with $100,000 as a down payment, if the value of the home declines by 30%, the home is worth just $350,000 but the investor still must pay interest and principal on the full value of the $400,000 loan. Should the amount the investor gets in rent decline too; the result could be default on the property. If the investor was using the cash flow from that property to pay the mortgage on other properties, the loss of income could produce a domino effect that can end with an entire portfolio in foreclosure over one bad loan on one property.

Buy and Hold Versus Flipping

This really should not be phrased as a competition; after all, flipping is a great business, and there is no reason why flipping and holding must be mutually exclusive. There are reasons why people flip property.

Some people purchase a unit or a house in an up-and-coming neighbourhood that they are banking on to increase in value. If you buy in a new development, you are hoping that there will be features that will attract higher-end homebuyers who will want the luxury features and space offered in these areas. If all goes well, you could make a nice profit when you are ready to sell. However, if something goes wrong, faulty budgeting, timing issues, a crime spike in that up-and-coming neighbourhood – you could be stuck with a house you can't get rid of because your property has gone down in value and you do not want to sell or simply that your property does not attract buyers.

Some other people look for fixer-uppers and foreclosure units. That was just what I did in the beginning. With my foreclosure unit in Richmond, I put in a bit of money to clean up the place and I eventually sold it off at a great price. Never overcapitalize on an investment. Customizing your renovations by sinking thousands or millions into a home renovation on many occasions will not reflect on a higher purchase price.

Something that may be of worth to you may be worthless to the next owner.

In Hong Kong during the early real-estate boom in early to mid-2000s, you could have flipped a place without doing any additional work on it. Some flippers could buy homes, hold on to them for a few months, and sell it off at a profit. Some transactions have even been held for as little as a few days before changing hands.

However with the current government measures imposed by the Hong Kong government, the possibility of flipping property is no longer profitable due to the Special Stamp Duty (SSD) on residential properties in Hong Kong. Units that are sold within the first three years of sale either by an individual or a company (regardless of where it is incorporated) will be subject to a Special Stamp Duty.

Units held for less than 36 months will be charged a Seller's Stamp Duty	
Holding period	
6 months or less	20%
More than 6 months but for 12 months or less	15%
More than 12 months but for 24 months or less	10%
More than 24 months but for 36 months or less	10%

The Power of Leveraging

Buy and Hold for the Long Run

Real estate is one of those few assets where we can build wealth by borrowing. Moreover, we can borrow for long periods. There are not too many investments where investors can get the comfort of a 20 to 30 year lending period.

I am a firm believer of buy and hold with my investments. Someone once asked John Jacob Astor, the famous real estate investor and America's first multi-millionaire, while on his deathbed if he could start over what he would do differently. Astor responded, "Yes, I would have bought every inch of Manhattan."

While the anecdote may be apocryphal, it highlights what many investors have said: "Every time I've sold a property, I've ended up regretting it." Even my first unit I own and sold in Richmond, I regret selling that unit because I have now lost my little footprint in Vancouver and trying to buy that back, I have to shell out a lot more money.

There are, of course, exceptions, and obviously, this doesn't apply to flippers. But in general, I firmly believe that buy and hold is the **best way** yet to become independently wealthy. While the average renter may have a net worth of $50,000, the minimum net worth a homeowner would have on the west side of Hong Kong island would be at least HKD$5 million. Keep in mind that all it takes to be counted as a homeowner is the purchase of one single 400 square foot unit. Try multiplying that a few times over and see what happens.

Buy and hold real estate investment has multiple, significant advantages over other investments :-

1) Passive Income

Most investments offer either a consistent return (i.e. annuities) or the potential for equity appreciation (i.e. stocks). Real estate offers both. Good buy and hold investments offer positive cash flow from rents that not only offset the expenses and debt service, but also provide a monthly income.

The average annuity only pays out 3.27% per year. A halfway decent buy and hold investor can beat that any day. Holding real estate can be a very passive investment that provides returns much higher than could be obtained through other passive investments (ie. stocks, bonds etc.). With the ability to outsource property management, accounting, etc., investors can still make good returns while playing a very hands off roll in the investment.

2) Depreciation

Flipping is a great business, but one of the biggest cons is that the taxman always gets his share. Not so with buy and hold. In some countries like Hong Kong, the government has applied measures like the SSD (Seller's Stamp Duties) to reduce or eliminate the incentives of flipping properties. In some other countries, you are allowed to write off the value of any property over 27.5 years. This depreciation counts as negative income, but it is only negative on paper since the costs of keeping a property in good condition can be paid for out of the rental income. Thus, the depreciation "losses" wipe out the positive cash flow from the property and remove any tax obligation.

3) Hedge Against Inflation

Many analysts believe inflation is coming (if not already here). Owning real estate and using leverage (especially at these low interest rates) is a great way to hedge against coming inflation. If prices rise, so will the cost of housing … owning an asset that rises with the tide is a great way to protect your wealth.

4) Equity Build Up

Real estate is the easiest investment to leverage (more on that later). With a mortgage, unfortunately, comes the obligation to pay it back. Fortunately, the cash flow mentioned above allows investors to pay back that mortgage without spending any of their own money. Instead, the tenant pays for it. Furthermore, each month — assuming you don't have an interest-only loan — part of the principle is paid off, too. Right off the bat, with a 30-year amortization, about 15 to 25% (depending on the interest rate) of each loan payment pays off the principle of the loan and adds to the equity you have in the property.

5) Increasing Rents

Very few would speculate that housing rents will decrease over time. Most analysts have already stated that rents are expected to increase over the coming years. Owning real estate not only allows you to lock in housing prices and interest rates that are at all-time lows, it also provides you with an opportunity to increase future cash flows by increasing rents … thus increasing your ROI (return on investment) in future years.

6) Appreciation

Real estate, like any other asset, can go up or down in value. Many have been scared off by the crash in 2007. However, a look at the long-term history of real estate prices is encouraging. When you look at real estate over the long haul, it is accurate to assume some level of appreciation in your real estate holdings. Yes there are market cycles where values rise quickly or fall quickly but by and large, real estate is an asset class that appreciates. The trend is consistently up. In fact, over

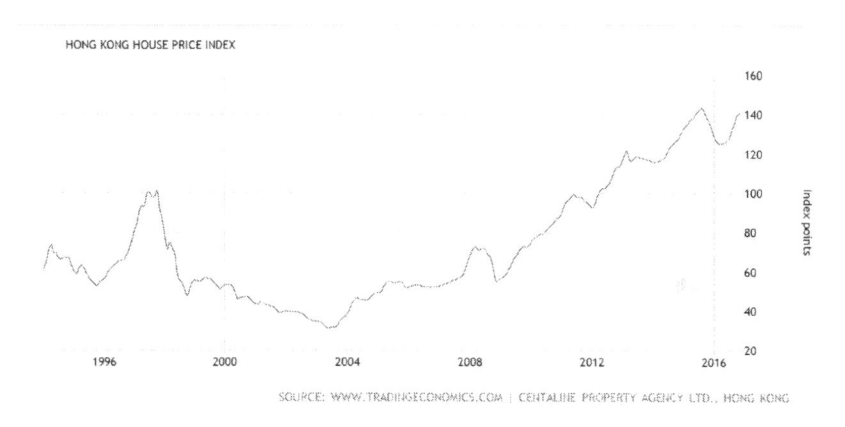

HONG KONG HOUSE PRICE INDEX

SOURCE: WWW.TRADINGECONOMICS.COM | CENTALINE PROPERTY AGENCY LTD., HONG KONG

the past 40 years, real estate has gone up an average of 4.62% per year. You can see from the Hong Kong House Price Index, the price of real estate has consistently risen since 2003.

The combination of accelerating equity pay down (with each payment, you pay more principle and less interest), and appreciation means that the investor's equity in any given property will grow exponentially the longer they hold it.

Some have pointed out that the stock market generally has a better return than real estate. This is true, but deceptive. That's because real estate is generally leveraged at a rate of four or five to one. Stocks, on the other hand, are rarely leveraged much, especially after the massive losses taken by those "buying on the margin" before the Great Depression. Which leads me to the next point:

7) Leverage

If you invest $20,000 into the stock market, and it goes up 10%, you've made $2000. If you invest that same money into real estate, you can buy a $100,000 property with an $80,000 loan. Let's say it only goes up 5%. Well, you've made $5000. Or in other words, you've made a 25% return!

So the fact that the stock market has a higher return on average is immaterial since your returns with real estate are based on a much higher amount than your principal investment.

One might think this makes real estate more risky than stocks, but that isn't so either. Stock prices are typically more volatile than real estate prices. Indeed, a buy and hold investor

The Power of Leveraging

who invests right can even make it through major downturns like the recent crisis (which saw stocks drop as much as real estate, by the way) with the positive cash flow from the property. Today, housing prices have even returned to pre-recession levels in many markets.

In the long run, real estate and stocks both go up. So if you can survive the downturns with positive cash flow, you'll be just fine in the long term.

Remember, I did all this while still working as a teacher on a modest fixed salary. Yet I was still able to accumulate the properties I have now by leveraging. From my very first unit in Richmond, Canada I leveraged capital from the sale to buy the unit on Caine road. The market sale price in 2006 was $2.38 million. I put down a 30% (HKD$714,000) towards the purchase and since then, the property has risen above $6 million dollars giving me a gross yield on initial purchase of 10% per annum. That is about 151% or 8.75% per annum compound.

With the rise in value, I leveraged some of the equity out of that unit and used the capital to reinvest. I understood the risks involved. The key risk is the ability to service debt out of income, either personal income, or rental income for investment properties. I just had to make sure that if my rental income did not cover the monthly mortgage, management fees and expenses, that I was able to cover it with my income.

Also when I borrow I need to understand the various debt repayment options. Debt repayments are a function of interest rates and lengths of repayment. A longer repayment period reduces the monthly repayment amount, but that means paying more interest over the life of the mortgage. It also means increasing your interest rate risks substantially if you have a floating rate mortgage. If you have a floating mortgage, you must allow for some breathing space, especially with interest rates as low as they are today. Could you afford to make the payment if the monthly mortgage payments doubles?

8) Retirement Income

For those investors that look at real estate investing as a very long-term proposition, the potential to retire on rental income is very real. I know many investors who have owned real estate for multiple decades as a retirement strategy and ended up very wealthy as a result.

Over a 20-30 year period of time, investors can own numerous properties outright and create a net worth well into the millions. Additionally, the cash flow that can be generated from properties that no longer have mortgages can be very nice supplements to pensions, social security, and retirement funds.

Chapter Five:
The Rules of the Game

If I had not listened and worked with the right individuals who were already in the market when I was starting out, without their knowledge, experience and guidance I would not be where I am financially today. Over many years, my friends and I have spent hours debating and discussing the pros and cons of purchasing property in various locations around the world.

Whenever I have any kind of casual, business or formal meeting and someone finds out that my business is property, I can guarantee that 99% of the time, someone will have something to say about property. Whether it is a property that they are trying to sell, whether they are trying to find a new place to lease or whether they are interested in buying a new investment. Someone always has something to say about real estate.

The Rules of the Game

Many people would ask me questions because they are sincerely curious about my opinion about various aspects of the market and some other people very happily volunteer their opinions about where they suspect the direction of the market is going. I've highlighted some of these questions and some comments that individuals have given me and tried to answer them as best as I can.

Chapter Six:
I don't feel comfortable buying property in a different country.

I, myself, asked the same question to Alan when he first asked me whether I would consider investing in a different place other than where I am residing. Of course if you have never done something like this before, the idea would be a bit daunting. For most people, the more traditional reason for purchasing a home is first to buy for the purpose of self-use. After that, if you are still thinking of buying more property, then you are buying as an investor.

So what do you normally do when you are in the market to buy a property? Well, you naturally find a property agent and physically go house hunting. The thought of buying a place unseen because it is in a different country that you may or may not be familiar with would be quite unnerving. How could you

I don't feel comfortable buying property in a different country.

possible agree to invest into something without actually seeing it?

I can take this question a few ways. When you buy mutual funds, whether they are in precious metals, emerging markets, or a European growth fund for example, what do you see of these funds? How much information can you research before you put money down on these purchases? Yes, you understand that your money is going towards a general fund and a fund manager will be looking after your money. How much experience does the fund manager who is in charge of your investment have? You may be given some sort of holding certificate for these funds and an annual report of their performance but how closely are you able to follow this type of investment? How much control do you have?

The key reason why you are probably uncomfortable in buying property in a different country is that you are not sure how much control you have. You may not know the steps to buying and you may not be familiar with the location. In Hong Kong, investors are inundated with property investment companies who peddle their wears to entice people to purchase property in their neck of the woods. Many of these companies offer investors first hand property in the UK, USA and Australia.

I've been an investor in these companies myself but of course how can you pick the right investment for you?

Yes, in order to purchase property, you will need a lot more capital to get into the property market but that is not any different to many other large investment plans. More importantly, you need a buyer's agent or a property agent you can trust. With property, you are buying tangible assets. You are buying brick, steel and glass. Yes in regards to geography if you are in Hong Kong it is not impossible to get on a plane and fly over to your target location to have a look at the location and study the local area. But with a buyer's agent, they will do the research for you. They will tell you where the new transport lines will be built and they will know what plans the city council will have in the coming years in regards to city development. I've never suggested that you needed to do this all on your own.

After I established my properties in Hong Kong, I started to look into investing overseas. With the properties I bought and sold in the UK, all I saw of the units were the floor plans, aerial maps and development documentation. The banks approved of my mortgage and the solicitors handled the sales transaction. Once it was completed, the property agent would arrange handover. They would send me photos of the unit so at

I don't feel comfortable buying property in a different country.

least I saw what I just purchased and they would find a suitable tenant. For five years all I saw was a monthly deposit of rental income in my bank account. In the end, when I sold the unit, everything was again handled through email and telephone correspondence and I received a nice balance in my bank account when the sale completed.

From that point onward, whenever I buy property, I am more comfortable now to judge my purchases with maps, studying the proximity to the local transportation system and get data on the expected rental income I would get for the unit in that particular area. Some would even suggest to not even look at the pictures but only look at the numbers.

A good buyer's agent should also be able to tell you what the potential yield and the potential growth is for that area - whether there is any city council plans to improve or gentrify the community. Of course with Alan, you also get the English understanding of the culture and economics of the country. You want to look for cities that have cultural and economic diversity. Does this country have a strong currency? And if so, can it withstand the down swings in the market?

Some property market sceptics predict that the market right now is abnormally high so they plan to wait for the bubble to pop before they are ready to get into the property market. That is their choice to wait but looking at historical patterns of house price indexes, when you're ready to get in, you should get in.

There are more factors and measures that have been implemented in our global economy to prevent global catastrophes from happening. Even though with BREXIT we saw a drop in the sterling, we won't get to the point that people will be picking gold off the streets of London any time soon because you suspect property prices might plummet. Before you predict certain cities to fall into economic crisis understand that countries like the United Kingdom, Hong Kong and Canada have enough checks and balances to curtail economic catastrophe from happening.

I want to buy a property to help my family out.

Chapter Seven:
I want to buy a property to help my family out.

As much as we all want to help our family because we love them, we need to remind ourselves why we are investing in property in the first place. Do you want to buy property because we are social workers? Or do we want to become investors. Now, along the way if you help some people – all the better. But remember – helping people is NOT the reason you are doing this. You are doing this for profit – not to be your own social organization. You can volunteer your time and energy towards your favourite charity but don't do it through this method.

I don't want to sound like Uncle Scrooge in this matter and bah humbug your idea to help Cousin Jim who is struggling to make ends meet back home but I need to steer you away from making these mistakes. We are trying to manage your wealth, not theirs.

Whenever you invest in property, like all other sorts of investment you should not have any emotional connections to them. The idea of investments is to get in when you see an opportunity and get out when the time is right to get out. Of course property investment isn't as easy to get in and to get out of as stocks. It is a steady form of investment that I've grown to be more accustomed to because I have little time in my day to be vigorously watching stocks go up and down.

You don't want to involve family or friends when you make investment decisions. If you buy a place and allow Cousin Jim to move in as a tenant, the idea may sound great at first because you now have a family member who could possibly look after your place and will pay rent towards your mortgage. But what happens when after a few months, Cousin Jim falls into hardship, loses his job and tells you that he won't be able to make next month's rent? Or that since you're family, he wanted to ask whether you can lower your monthly rent because he spent too much money last month taking his kids on that summer vacation they have always wanted to go on. What would you do then? Are you prepared to take the financial hit as a result? Is he your responsibility?

I want to buy a property to help my family out.

Can you so easily evict Cousin Jim because he can't pay next month's rent? How about the month after that? Or will you just have to offer to pay those few months, reduce his rent or even allow him to stay for free until he gets back on his feet? You'll probably get pressure from the family and because if you are not there, your family would not want to get involved or take sides. It would be even harder to ask him to leave because there is more weight on your shoulders to be the better member in the family who is helping out the family.

Another scenario would be, if Cousin Jim has been a great tenant and has paid his rent on time, after one year, could you so easily tell him that you will be raising his rent?

Make the smarter choice and do not involve your family or friends in your investment because you should not have any emotional ties to your investments when you come to the point that you want to cash in.

You need to be unemotional in your decisions so your relationships with your tenants should be strictly professional. I've had to face moments when I had to ask tenants to leave because they were not paying their rent or because I had just sold the unit. Trust me, it is much easier to talk to someone you have no emotional ties with.

Even with other forms of investments, you don't see people having emotional ties with their stocks or bonds when it comes time for them to sell. You shouldn't have any issues selling off your property investments when it comes time that you need to.

I hate to sound cold but you are investing and not running a charity. You should never rent out to friends or family members unless there is a clear understanding of where the line is drawn between landlord and tenant. Your tenant's economic condition is not your fault or your problem. You are not responsible for your tenants finances or lack of it. It is neither because of you that they may not be in the best position financially nor because of how much you may raise their rent. You are not responsible for their wellbeing. They are!

You are trying to build yourself some financial freedom and while you now are looking for that opportunity consider what you need to do to get there. While you are buying property, you are technically trying to establish a business. You are in this to make money for yourself and/or the people you care about. Why else would you go through all of this trouble? Again – if you want to HELP people, volunteer or contribute to charity.

I want to buy a property to help my family out.

It is much easier to ask a tenant to leave if you have no emotional ties to them. You will find others who will gladly pay you your asking rental price. The current tenants are not a permanent fixture of the property and cannot be treated that way.

Chapter Eight:
Who's going to look after my property when I'm not there?

There are property management companies that will help foreign investors collect your keys at completion, help you furnish the unit, find an appropriate tenant, and manage the property for you. Their fees may range between 11-18%, which is a wide range, which is why you need to shop around for the company you are happy with. This fee can be a small dent in your annual yield but this enables you to have the ability to remain at an arm's length away from being at your tenant's beck and call. If there are issues with the property you know there is someone who will address them should they arise.

The reason why I use property management companies is to avoid emotional hang ups altogether by having a barrier between you and your tenant. Having a property management company in place to take your orders from day one of ownership

Who's going to look after my property when I'm not there?

enables them to deal with all the baggage that comes along with being a landlord. It simply takes you out of this emotional equation.

By having a management company in place you are more objective and can make decisions from a business standpoint, not an emotional standpoint because sometimes tenants will try to pull wool over your eyes or try to turn it into something you are responsible for.

I once had a tenant drop a heavy cosmetic bottle over my bathroom sink and cracked it. Nonchalantly, she called up my property manager to advise me to replace it. I asked my manager why I had to pay for this when it was she who broke my sink. The tenant tried to explain that the sink was of poor quality and that a small jar lightly fell in and cracked it. Well, I said that since she felt that the sink was of poor quality then she should have been more careful to not have cracked it.

In general, tenants are protected against minor "wear and tear" of the unit but a broken sink? Com'on, sorry, she had to replace it. Thankfully, I didn't have to do the dirty work and told my property manager to tell her the bad news.

Some of you may prefer having someone you know like a family member or friend to manage the property for you. That may be good for some people but I personally prefer not to involve family in my investments just to keep things clear with what is considered family and what is considered business. Maybe you pay the management fee to your family and they manage it for you. You arrange this with them.

A second tenant complained through my property manager to say that the Internet connection port broke off. It was loose when she first used it and now it broke off entirely and she can't use the wired Internet anymore. So she's asking me to hire someone to fix it.

Growing up, I've been fortunate enough to have a father who was a very hands-on working man who knew how to do gardening, wood-working, electrical wiring and mechanical work on the car. Some of it did rub off on me. In Canada, you need to be more hands on with your own home. It's not cheap to call in an electrician or a plumber. An electrician will come in, look at the work, quote you $500 Canadian dollars and take only ten minutes to fix it. You tend to learn quickly how to fix things around the house without needing to call in a professional.

When I received this email, I was sitting at dinner in Hong Kong, while this tenant was in London. I'm looking at the

Who's going to look after my property when I'm not there?

email I received from my property manager and I'm wondering, "Do people not have simple problem solving skills?" I would have gone out to the local electrical store, asked for the replacement part and repaired it myself. Would I have really needed to bother the property manager who then had to send me an email asking me to hire someone all the way here from Hong Kong to fix her Internet plug? Sure I'll be there in about 15 hours. Let me book my plane ticket right away!

Well, I fired an email back to the property manager to ask her to ask the tenant what steps has she taken to either find the cost to hire an electrician to fix the problem? Or whether they are able to fix it themselves? You need to be prepared to give your tenants a little nudge in order for them to learn how to problem solve by themselves.

Yes I am the landlord but I won't come to your beck and call when you don't know how to turn on the gas stove. Sometimes you'll have tenants whom you will never hear anything about and you'll have ones who don't know how to clear the drain. Just because they are paying rent to you, there are lines you need to draw as to what things you will do for them.

Chapter Nine:
Airbnb

One of the hottest topics individuals who are involved with property want to know more about is the online market place and hospitality service, Airbnb. This company enables people to list or rent short-term lodgings including vacation rentals, apartment rentals, homestays, hostel beds, or hotel rooms. They are merely a brokerage that receives commission fees from both guests and hosts in conjunction with every booking.

A host can create a listing, determine the price, and add descriptions for the residence, amenities, available dates, cancellation policies and any house rules they may have. They upload photos of their lodging and interested parties can message the property owner directly through Airbnb to ask questions and inquire about booking. The website will then facilitate the online payments from the guest to host which is processed 24 hours after check-in.

The host has the option of asking for security deposits, cleaning fees and prospective guests are required to provide verified IDs before booking. They can also use the travel guide feature to provide in-depth information for restaurants and entertainment around their neighbourhood.

Most people who host on Airbnb use the service to let out their home while they are away on vacation. Some let out part of their space in order to supplement their income. Others let out their homes on a more consistent basis.

I have had many clients inquire about Airbnb and want to know more about how they can get started with setting up a listing and whether it is better than letting out their homes on a more long term basis. They ask me whether it is more beneficial to let through Airbnb than going the more traditional route of long term leasing.

If they want to talk about yields and return, is it more profitable to do short term leasing rather than long term leasing. How much more (or less) could I earn by running an Airbnb vacation rental, as compared with traditional landlording? Now, I'm going to be speaking strictly with the assumption that you would like to do this in Hong Kong and not anywhere else. I have done long-term rentals of my units and occasionally I have put my units on Airbnb for short term leasing for various reasons.

I cannot say this enough as a landlord and as a real estate agent but the majority of visiting tourists want a place that has easy access to public transportation. However, there are many other individuals who look on Airbnb for places that have other appeals such as beachfront locations, resort locations or just quieter areas. I have in the past rented out all of my units on Airbnb and all of them have done very well for different reasons.

My subject property

In 2012, I bought a small unit in the new gentrified area of Sai Ying Pun. The unit was left to a cousin of mine by my late grandmother and he did not want to keep the property so I swept in and bought it from him.

Fook Moon Building, 56-72 Third Street, Sai Ying Pun

Purchased	Nov 2012	2016 HSBC Bank Valuation	$4.23
Price	$3.00M	Estimated Rent	$14K per month
Saleable Area (sf)	305	Age of Building	35 years
Total Growth/ Per Annum Compound	41% Total 8.97% pa	Gross Yield on Initial Purchase	6% per annum

Brief: Long term investment property, mature residential area, central expat location

Property: Leasehold - 1 bedroom conversion in high demand location in Sai Ying Pun, right next to the SYP escalators. Great location to bars and restaurants. One block from the MTR exit. Excellent studio with large bathroom and kitchenette. Ideal unit for short term leasing.

The location was a prime location. It was just one block from the new MTR station and right on the corner of where new bars and restaurants were emerging. It was an extremely run down unit but with a complete overhaul I leased it out to a long-term tenant. My experience with that tenant did not go well because right from the beginning she was late on her rent. Eventually we ended up in small claims court for over a year from which I won the case and victoriously evicted the tenant.

After that experience I was angry and frustrated for having dealt with such a difficult tenant but this is clearly one of the drawbacks of being a property owner and an investor who manages their own property. The ordeal left me very apprehensive in looking for another tenant soon after so I decided to try Airbnb for a while and maybe later find a more suitable tenant.

Even though the unit was extremely small, it was perfect as an Airbnb unit because of its location. The renovation work that I had done to the unit was geared for the weary traveller. The unit was made specifically like a hotel suite with a large queen bed, small wardrobe, large sofa that converted into a sofa bed, TV and a kitchenette. The bathroom was quite spacious as well. I decided to keep the kitchen as a small kitchenette because situated in Sai Ying Pun and targeting visitors, most would be eating out rather than staying home to cook. Still I did provide a small induction cooker, some pots and pans if guests wanted to make a simple fry up in the morning.

I provided towels, linens, duvets and pillows. The bathroom was stocked with soap, shampoo, and toilet paper. So you can image that there is definitely more work that needs to be done with running Airbnb units. I had to schedule my turnover days but with accessing the units, I installed a keyless entry lock so my guests could self check-in.

Traditionally, a long-term tenant pays between HKD$12,000 to $14,000/month but now because I am offering it as an Airbnb vacation rental, will I make money hand-over-fist? Or will I lose my shirt?

Occupancy

My biggest fear is my vacancy rates. As any landlord can tell you, nothing is more expensive than vacancy. Most guests book on Airbnb because they are able to find a room that is more affordable than hotels. Some decide to stay in order to experience the more home-like feel of staying in someone's home. Some travellers choose Airbnb in order to gain a different experience all together.

Because of the location of the unit being just one block from the subway station, my occupancy rate was close to 93%. I had a very competitive rate, I charged a cleaning fee and extra if there were more than two guests because I would have to set out extra linens and towels to prepare the sofa bed. During high seasons the system prices the unit higher while lower seasons it would modify the pricing so that my unit would still look very attractive for booking.

Guest Quality

There is one risk that is even more expensive than vacancy: destruction. If your guest trashes your home, you could (theoretically) lose a lot of money to repair and replace. There are many newspaper reports of horror stories of Airbnb guests who throw wild parties and cause immense damage to the host's home. Fortunately, my apartment is basically too small to host big gala parties. I usually have tourists who are travelling through, business people in town, and people who have family and friends in town they are visiting.

Issues

In fairness, I need to share the downsides, as well. Primarily: vacation rentals are *waaayyyy* less outsourcing-friendly than I'd anticipated. Here's my initial thinking:

Step 1: Develop systems and processes. Example: "Here's the cleaning checklist: wash sheets, empty trash cans, dust, mop, vacuum, etc."

Step 2: Hire housecleaners to manage the turnover.

Step 3: Maintain a "supply closet" filled with toilet paper, soap, shampoo and hand wash and detergent etc., to reduce the number of trips to the store.

Step 4: Communicate with guests through the smartphone app.

Step 5: Have a mostly-hands-off business. I will still field inquiries, which would take about 30 minutes per week (5-10 minutes/day, a couple days per week), but the rest would be systematized.

Or so I thought. Reality had different plans. I've created these processes for my rental properties (as a traditional landlord), and it worked like a charm. My traditional rental properties – after they've been renovated – are totally passive. I just kick back and watch the money roll in. (Buying and renovating the properties can be an ordeal, but the aftermath is glorious.) Unfortunately, vacation rentals are not as hands-off. Here are some of the issues I've had to troubleshoot:

Issue #1: Consumables.

Luckily, since I fitted the home to be more like a hotel room, I only had basics for the bathroom and kitchen. I supplied the consumables like toilet paper, hand soap, shampoo and body wash, dishwashing liquid, and trashcan liners. These are "consumables" – meaning that they need constant restocking. I figured I would keep a "supply closet" within the apartment. Bad idea.

As it turns out, *people steal from supply closets.* I am a little flabbergasted that someone would pay HKD$1800 for a three day stay in Hong Kong and take with them all ten rolls of toilet paper – but that's how life shakes out. What is strange is that nobody steals the "indefensible" stuff – pots, pans, the TV. That is too flagrant. But "consumables" seem to be viewed in some morally-ambiguous zone.

This doesn't happen with all guests, of course. Only a few. But after you lose enough toilet paper, you start thinking that maybe you should keep your supply closet locked up.

Issue #2: Maintenance and Repair

Of course, the restocking issue is not a huge deal. Just create a checklist for the housekeeper, which includes "Check quantities of soap/sponges/etc. Resupply as needed." List each specific item, with a check-box next to it. House the supply closet in a locked trunk, and include a set of keys. Voila – you're done. That would be great … if I could find a reliable housekeeper.

Luckily in Hong Kong, hired help is more readily available with few issues. Check-out is at 11 a.m., which means realistically, people leave at 12 noon. Check-in is at 3 p.m., which means realistically, people arrive at 1 p.m. That leaves a tight window of time to process the turnover. My hired help is usually punctual and is flexible whenever my guests ask for a late check-out. It is when there are more issues with the apartment.

Occassionaly it is when something more serious happens like, the heater breaks down, a bursted pipe under the sink, or of course with Murphy's Law, the air conditioning unit breaks down during the hottest period of the year.

Moments like this when I'm panicking and calling multiple repairmen to see who can come the soonest to help me address the issue. Most of the time I am in town to deal with the matters or that my helper is able to assist but more serious issues really require a handyman or someone who knows how to deal with these types of home repair. When I am away, I leave praying that no issues will arise while I am away from Hong Kong.

Issue #3: Growing Pains

No one knows your home as well as you know so there are always some growing pains in trying to anticipate what a guest may expect from your home and what you know your place is capable of.

Hot water supply. In Hong Kong, each unit is self contained with things like heating units and cooling units. Some water heaters are instantaneous and others are a small tank in the ceiling that only provide hot water for a limited time.

Two of my units have a small electric heater in the ceiling and I was getting numerous complaints that the hot water kept running out too quickly because usually in hotels, the supply of hot water is continuous. To solve the situation, I removed some of the panels from the ceiling so guests saw that there is a tank so if they used all the water in the tank, it will take some time for it to heat up. Problem solved. No more complaints of not enough hot water.

Also, if they forget to turn the hot water switch on, the tank would not heat up. Solution, I had to stick labels around the house so they knew which switch to flip for which machine.

Insects in Hong Kong. Hong Kong's climate is a subtropical climate. That means that besides 7.4 million peoplie living here, there are even more insects, snakes and rodents who call this place their home.

We keep our home clean. We tell our guests to keep food in the kitchen or dining but insects still crawl in from the outside. Much of this in unpreventable because of the climate.

I'd get guests who come in from colder climates where cockroaches and geckos don't exist and I get calls that they just saw a cockroach in the kitchen when they came back by the end of the day.

I would ask them, "How many did you see? You only saw one? Wow, you're lucky!" I put a sign up to explain that the insects are a part of Hong Kong and left a bottle of bug repellant on the table.

Another place I had to advise them that in the evening they should close all the windows before they go to sleep because mice may crawl in from outside to forage for food.

Sometimes I would have a guest who does not know how to change the channels on the cable TV. I had one guest contact me to complain that the shower hose broke or another guest could not figure out how to work the dimmer of the light. I had two guys from Tel Aviv and somehow they had tampered with the keyless entry lock and had locked themselves in. Of course that was the hour that my phone battery died so I decided to enjoy an uninterrupted meal to come home to turn my phone back on to see ten messages from my guest calling for help!

I had another guest and her family fly in from Singapore and call me in the evening telling me that none of their devices were able to log onto the internet. I called the company and even asked the previous guest if there were any issues with the service. They said no.

So in the end, I had to travel all the way there, bring my laptop and voilà, the Internet was indeed working. I never figured out why their devices were not able to get on the Internet but situations like this is a real hassle and can be frustrating to say the least. Sometimes, these house calls would take a big chunk of your time away from your regularly scheduled program.

Some complaints are rational yet there are many where you wonder how on earth do they manage their daily lives.

Some guests have the same expectations that your place of lodging should still be like a stay at the Four Seasons. Some ask for daily housekeeping and whether the towels will be refreshed daily. The answer is no.

I had one call around 10:30 in the evening. I was in bed already and somehow the Korean guest had clogged the shower drain with her hair and water was spilling onto the floor. She asked…no actually, she demanded that I come over to address the issue immediately or call a professional plumber. I politely advised her to remove whatever debris was blocking the drain and give the plunger a few pumps on the drain. What more would you think anyone would be able to do at this time of night? Would a plumber be able to do more than you taking a plunger and pumping the drain to clear the clog?

Some of your guests do not have the right expectations. They are staying in someone's home so expectations do need to be set. Some guests you never hear a peep from. They arrive and leave without any trouble or if there was, they would simply let me know to address it later when you come for turnover. Others do not know even how to unlock the door, turn on the light or readjust the toilet seat if by some possibility it has been push out of alignment!

Short term leasing requires more attention and it is definitely not considered passive income because you can never just leave it alone.

There have been times when the question of, "Is this really worth it?" crossed my mind or whether I should change my unit back to a long term tenant. Then I crunch the numbers, look at my monthly revenue and think, *"Hell yeah."*

Income

The monthly rent I was collecting on the unit when it was being rented long term was roughly HKD$12,000/month. I was responsible for the management fees and government rates. The tenant paid for their own utilities. Now that the unit is on Airbnb, I still pay for the fees I was paying before but I am also responsible for the water, electricity, gas but also for the cable TV and WIFI Internet access.

My monthly expenses included laundry, supplies and the cost of hiring help. But for the first three months, I reached high occupancy and averaged about HKD $18,000/month. During peak travel seasons, the monthly income will be more and low seasons it would be less. The electricity bill will be usually higher in the summer because the air conditioners would be used more but I was doing 50% better managing the property on a short term basis.

Which Method is Better?

Is Airbnb better than long term leasing? It depends. No investment is "good" or "bad" in a vacuum. Every investment should be compared to the *next best alternative*. In this case, the "next best" is the rent I'd collect from a traditional one-year lease. I **was earning 50% more per month on Airbnb rather than landlording over a traditional tenant.**

I noticed that because of the type of guests I was getting, my apartment was getting less wear and tear. Most of the time, guests were out visiting the city and they tended to eat out. Because I set a required minimum of nights, I was able to space out the frequencies of needing to do turnover on the units and guests would not stay too long that they would try to personalize the space.

Long term tenants tend to put up wall hangings, damage the apartment with scuff marks on the walls due to normal wear and tear or appliances would break down on occasion.

How much extra work does Airbnb require?

Besides the occassional replacement of light bulbs and cleaning of air conditioning units. Not much as long as you keep everything in tip-top shape, you won't need a lot of maintenance.

Answering inquiries is easy – I reply to emails through my phone or laptop. It is about as much of a hassle as checking Twitter or posting to Facebook. Time commitment: negligible.

Meeting guests is unnecessary. My units have keyless entry locks so I give the codes out to them before they arrive. Some usually do not read their instructions but majority of the check-ins run very smoothly. The Airbnb website automatically emails the guests directions. Result: The check-in process is totally hands-off.

Playing tour-guide is automated. I have a "Welcome Guide" that offers the guests tips on the best places nearby to eat, drink, shop, etc., along with directions on how to get there by walking, train, bus and taxi. The "welcome guide" also includes tips about the apartment (e.g. "this is how to operate the stove") and the Wifi password.

The biggest hassle is turnover. Cleaning the apartment takes about 1.5 to two hours. If there are any issues that need my attention, I usually have to address them within that changeover window and that requires a bit of coordination, preparation and timing so if you are managing your units by yourself, it would be wiser that your daytime job is flexible that allows you to get away whenever you need.

What location should I choose to start my Airbnb business?

Location, location, location! Yes, I am coming back to that again. I just described to you how my Airbnb unit situated one block from the Sai Ying Pun MTR did. For a little unit like that, it has done phenomenally well. Most travellers prefer staying closer to transportation routes that are easily accessible. However, I have another example of an Airbnb unit that is doing just as well for different reasons.

Units on the outlying islands of Hong Kong can do remarkably well for different reasons. In the past, my family would come and spend a month or two in Hong Kong once a year. So when they are here, they stay at our home and when they fly back to Vancouver, the unit was kept empty so if the place was not used for long periods of time the appliances and the furniture would being to deteriorate. Because of the sub tropical climate in Hong Kong, if a place is not used mould would form on the walls and the place would begin to suffer.

Airbnb gave me the flexibility to rent out the unit on a short-term basis, I was able to keep a home available for when family and friends come to stay. The revenue that comes from the leasing enables me to keep up with the necessary repairs to the place, enable me to give it a new coat of paint every few years, and service the appliances and air conditioning units on a regular basis. I am also able to arrange for the upkeep and renovation works that are needed.

Because the unit was on Park Island, I thought that the unit would not have much demand and the occupancy rate would be low because access to the island was only limited to the bus and ferry services. What I realized afterwards was that our home was the perfect place to book for other residents living on the island and visitors who come to see Disneyland.

There is only one hotel on the island so residents needed to find a place for their travelling friends and family to stay that is still close by. The son-in-laws were usually extremely happy to put their mother-in-laws at our unit instead of her staying with them!

Since the unit on Park Island is technically our home, we have photos and some personal items there. None are of too much value and our guests have treated our home with care and respect so I have not had too many upsetting incidences with difficult guests.

Usually I have families who stay rather than singles and couples. They are advised very clearly as to where the unit is situated and that the accessibility of the transportation routes are limiting but, the resort feel of the location and the access to the outdoor and indoor pools and beaches balances out the enjoyment of their stay.

Overall I have explained a small part of my experience with Airbnb. There are many other issues you need to be aware of before you put your home on Airbnb. Issues concerning tax declaration, tenancy laws, the conditions to your home insurance and the conditions of letting set out by your lending bank need to be addressed before you go ahead.

I want that holiday home I've dreamed about.

Chapter Ten:
I want that holiday home I've dreamed about.

So you want that holiday home where you can jet off to on the weekends in the Bahamas, Mexico, and/or Thailand. We've all dreamt of ourselves falling in love with a tropical island and wanting a piece of it.

Now that you have worked a steady job for a few years, you probably saved up some money and now you want to take that plunge and buy that holiday home. So now what? So every chance you are able to book holidays, for the first few years, you will go to your holiday home but will you keep going there after a few more years?

What are you going to do with your holiday home while you're not there? Will you rent it out? What happens in a few years when you decide that you don't want it anymore and you want to put it on the market for sale? How easy will it be to find a buyer? Are you able to consider this as an investment, something that you can profit from in the future?

Will this be considered? The definition of an investment is an asset or item that is purchased with the hope that it will generate income or will appreciate in the future. In an economic sense, an investment is the purchase of goods that are not consumed today but are used in the future to create wealth. In finance, an investment is a monetary asset purchased with the idea that the asset will provide income in the future or will be sold at a higher price for a profit.

Property is considered an investment because through time, the investor hopes to earn a profit from the rental income or from the capital growth of the property. If you are planning to buy a piece of property somewhere near a beach or somewhere that can be considered a holiday home, you still hope that you will make a profit when it comes time for you to sell?

If you buy a permanent holiday home, will you commit to spending every holiday there for the foreseeable future? Do you no longer want to visit other countries or regions? Will your children want to spend time there? Will you buy this place as an investment or are you simply treating this as consumption

I want that holiday home I've dreamed about.

expenditure, goods and services that you purchase for use by the household?

When you consider whether a piece of property is an investment, you need to look at whether it has the potential to be sold at a higher price for a profit in the future. So if you are buying property anywhere and you are looking to buy as an investment, you need to look at whether there is a strong secondary market because by the time you are ready to sell, you will be relying on a buyer to buy your second hand property.

Some countries, for example Thailand, have development projects that build lavish vacation villas all equipped with its own pool and latest "bells and whistles." These companies advertise and encourage foreigners to come buy these villas while offering management packages to take care of the villa while you are not there. They'll manage all the paperwork for you, so buying your dream summer home will seem extremely easy.

Most of these projects are off plan projects as well so again if you are unfamiliar with the developers, you may not know what you are buying. Sometimes the quality of the material they use to build these villas could be questionable. Will you understand all the maintenance and management bills you will need to pay for upkeep? How well do you understand the weather and climate in the country you are buying? If the house sits next to the beach, salt water in the air will increase the speed of deterioration of your home. If a house is built with poor quality materials, in a few years things it will look old and worn.

Due to warm humid climates, wooden doors and the cupboards may warp out of shape, the paint will chip, the tiles from the pool will start popping out and the electrical wiring will start eroding. Pretty soon, your villa will not look like the latest hottest villa on the block because your pool looks dated. What is more damning is that you may not be able to sell your villa off because there isn't enough interest in the secondary market for second hand holiday homes in Thailand. Everyone wants a new one.

If you are not going to retire and live in the villa, what are you going to do with it while you are not there? You will probably go three to four times in a year or you will invite friends and family to the villa but you probably let them stay for free or at a discount. You will spend money for upkeep and all your proceeds will probably go to the property management company who watches over it.

I want that holiday home I've dreamed about.

There are no guarantees that the tenants will be found. Short lettings require an efficient local manager to clean up and prepare it for the next tenants. They may need to fix the fridge, clean the pool, do the laundry, and tend to the gardening. Finding someone to do all of this can be difficult and expensive. Can you trust them with your instructions? More importantly, is there any growth or financial return on your investment when you decide to activate your exit strategy?

Is this a worthwhile investment plans? What is the potential capital growth in purchasing this property? Is there any financial return? Is this a wise investment?

I know an investor who bought a 20 million dollar baht (approximately $56,000.00 USD) villa in Koh Samui, Thailand. Because of this exact scenario of a poor secondary market, for the last ten years, he has been pouring money into the villa for just upkeep and maintenance. The villa has been for sale on the secondary market but it has been unable to attract anyone who would even consider paying the breakeven price for the cost of the home.

The wife is unwilling to accept taking a loss on the property so the buyer is at the point that he is begging for anyone to take it off his hands. Would you consider this a good ten-year investment? Has he made any capital gain on the property?

I heard this other story from an acquaintance I met a few years back. People love to talk about property whether it is good or bad news. This guy bought two beachfront apartment units somewhere in Thailand. He left them empty for a few months and comes back to discover squatters living in his apartments.

He calls the authorities but because he is a foreigner, the local police do not provide him with much help. He finds out that the people living in his home actually pay rent to a different individual who turns out to be part of the Thai mafia. The Thai police again were not too quick to get involved so this man was unable to ask the squatters to leave.

This is quite a sad story because for some people, buying property may be considered the biggest purchase in their life. For this guy, the Thai mafia took his two properties away and the Thai police did not help.

If you don't have a property management company that you trust, how would you manage the property from a distance? While you are slaving away in New York, London, Tokyo or Hong Kong to make the monthly payments towards your

I want that holiday home I've dreamed about.

holiday home, who is going to ensure the place is not going to be robbed or that all the furniture and furnishings will be there when you return? What happens if there is an issue? Will you just drop whatever you are doing and fly over to handle the problem?

The lesson to be learned here is that you can still buy property in foreign countries, but you need to understand the legal system and what protection you have being a foreigner in that country. If you buy property in countries where foreign investors are legally allowed to buy property, you want to know your civil rights and whether you are protected like any person living or investing in this country. Choose wisely where you buy because if there is any chance that you encounter trouble, there is a strong, fair governmental law enforcement that will protect you.

Chapter Eleven:
How do I buy Hong Kong property?

Before you decide that you want to invest in foreign property and specifically in Hong Kong property, you need to understand some of the restrictions of buying property as a foreigner.

Different countries have different restrictions. For example, land ownership in Thailand does not allow foreigners to own. Although there are ways to work around that. A foreign investor has two options. They can either purchase a 30-year leasehold or purchase the property through a limited company, or they can purchase apartments as long as there is 51% Thai ownership in the building.

In Australia, foreign investors can purchase property in Australia but only first-hand or new build properties. Only Australian citizens can purchase second hand property. Therefore, as a foreign investor, when it comes time to sell off

Are there any restrictions for foreign investors?

your property, you need to find a buyer with an Australian passport. This could limit the number of potential buyers you can approach.

In British Columbia, Canada, the provincial government now requires buyers who do not hold Canadian citizens or permanent residents of Canada to pay an extra 15% of the fair market value of any residential property they acquire.

Hong Kong Stamp Duties

The Hong Kong government imposes stamp duties on residential properties hoping to tame the soaring real estate prices in the world's least affordable major city.

If you are a Hong Kong permanent resident and buying residential (domestic use) property for the first time (that means that you are not holding any residential property under your own name, you qualify for the scale 2 of the Ad Valorem Stamp Duty. (see table below)

Lower Rates of Ad Valorem Stamp Duty (Scale 2)

Amount or value of the consideration or Value of the Property		Rate
Exceeds	Does not exceed	
	$2,000,000	$100
$2,000,000	$2,351,760	$100 + 10% of excess over $2,000,000
$2,351,760	$3,000,000	1.5%
$3,000,000	$3,290,320	$45,000 + 10% of excess over $3,000,000

$3,290,320	$4,000,000	2.25%
$4,000,000	$4,428,570	$90,000 + 10% of excess over $4,000,000
$4,428,570	$6,000,000	3.00%
$6,000,000	$6,720,000	$180,000 + 10% of excess over $6,000,000
$6,720,000	$20,000,000	3.75%
$20,000,000	$21,739,120	$750,000 + 10% of excess over $20,000,000
$21,739,120		4.25%

Besides residential properties there are other forms of immovable property in Hong Kong. These other forms of immovable properties include commercial or industrial properties which include business offices, warehouses and car parks. The stamp duty on the sale or transfer of immovable property (non residential) in Hong Kong is chargeable with ad valorem stamp duty (AVD) at higher rates (Scale) 1. The rates at Scale 1 are as follows:

Higher Rates of Ad Valorem Stamp Duty (Scale 1)

Amount or value of the consideration or Value of the Property		Rate
Exceeds	Does not exceed	
	$2,000,000	1.5%
$2,000,000	$2,176,470	$30,000 + 20% of excess over $2,000,000
$2,176,470	$3,000,000	3.0%
$3,000,000	$3,290,330	$90,000 + 20% of excess over $3,000,000
$3,290,330	$4,000,000	4.5%
$4,000,000	$4,428,580	$180,000 + 20% of excess over $4,000,000
$4,428,580	$6,000,000	6.00%
$6,000,000	$6,720,000	$360,000 + 20% of excess over $6,000,000
$6,720,000	$20,000,000	7.5%
$20,000,000	$21,739,130	$1,500,000 + 20% of excess over $20,000,000
$21,739,130		8.5%

Are there any restrictions for foreign investors?

If you are a Hong Kong permanent but you already own one residential property under your name in Hong Kong, you are liable to a 15% stamp duty towards any additional residential property purchase.

If you are a Hong Kong non-permanent resident or a company buying a property in Hong Kong, you must pay 15% stamp on the purchase price plus the 15% Ad Valorem Stamp Duty (AVSD). So if you are a non-permanent resident buying residential property, you will pay 30% more on top of the sale price for the unit.

In addition to the regular stamp duties charged on sale or transfer of immovable property, any residential property purchased either by an individual or a company (regardless of where it is incorporated), and resold within 24 months will be subject to a Special Stamp Duty (SSD).

Holding period	
6 months of less	20%
More than 6 months but for 12 months or less	15%
More than 12 months but for 24 months or less	10%
More than 24 months but for 35 months or less	10%

All these measures on foreign investors are attempts to discourage speculation of investors in hopes to stabilize the housing market. Property prices in Hong Kong have doubled and tripled over the past ten years amid rock-bottom interest rates and strong foreign demand, particularly among Mainland Chinese investors seeking higher returns and with a desire to move assets offshore.

This information can change at any time so what may be said today may not be what the rules are in a matter of months or even weeks. It is best to keep up to date with the information and contact your trusted real estate agent.

Consider the following 3-bedroom flat in Mid-levels. It has gross and saleable areas of 1,048 and 811 feet respectively. The asking price is HKD 14.8 million/ US$1.90m / £1.51 million which is eye-watering even before you add stamp duty (3.75% for a property of this value or an extra 30% if you are not a permanent resident – PR), agent fees of 1 to 2% and legal fees of around HKD $15,000 to $20,000, totalling approximately HKD15.523 million for a PR, or HKD19.408 million for a non-PR.

Mortgages

When it comes to mortgages, if you earn your income in Hong Kong, and are a first time homebuyer (not holding any residential properties at the time of application) you are eligible for the Mortgage Insurance Program (MIP) which allows for a 90% loan-to-value (LTV) ratio for properties below HKD 4 million.

Otherwise typical LTV ratios to buy property for personal use in Hong Kong are around 50-60%. Prime mortgage rates are around 5%, which means a real rate of 2.5-3%, with terms of usually 30 years. So all in all, mortgage terms are somewhat less attractive than in other prime markets due to high deposits required.

Now that a lot of the older buildings are reaching the ages of 50, the term of the mortgage is calculated by:

70 or 80 years minus 1) the age of the purchaser or 2) Year built whichever is shorter.

Where should I go for the best mortgage? This question goes back to my philosophy of leveraging. I prefer to not waste my time and energy going from bank to bank looking for the best mortgage deals. You may think that because you have been banking for a number of years at a particular large financial institution, you and your bank have developed some form of loyalty to each other. You may feel that because you, your partner, and your kids all have account numbers with them that they will immediately offer you the best deal.

Unfortunately, banks don't have the same loyalty towards their clients. Like all businesses, they go where the money is and so should you. If you were in the market for a new car, wouldn't you want to shop around and do your research to find the best price for the car you have in mind? Do you feel that the new car you get from one dealership would be of the same quality as the same new car from other dealership? Wouldn't you try as many ways to see if you can get a dealership to give you the best price you deserve?

You should have the mentality when you are in the market for a mortgage that the money one institution gives you is the same as the money another institution would give you. It all depends on the deal you get, whether it is the right length of term, the best interest rate and whether they include any more additional bonuses or credits.

I have had clients who have been stuck on the hope that if they have been banking with their large financial institution for so many years that somehow their bank will automatically give them everything they hoped for in a mortgage. Banks are just as competitive as other companies and it is their job to screen out qualified applicants and to be just as competitive for a client's money.

I go to whichever bank or financial institution offers the best deal. In order to make my job easier, I use mortgage brokers whenever I can. Remember that idea about leveraging?

Besides leveraging money, leverage your time and get other people to help you. Mortgage brokers have access to all the current rates for mortgages. They are continuously aware of the changes in lending and of all the bonuses banks are offering. They can quickly calculate your borrowing power to conclude how much you can afford for a new home purchase. Of course you can do all of this on your own, but why not take advantage of the people who are the experts in the field.

For example, the LTV ratio in Hong Kong for a second hand residential unit priced at HKD$10+ million (or US$1.29+ million/£1.03+ million) or above is 50%. That means that you need at least HKD$5 million (or US$643,000/£515,000) plus the appropriate amount of stamp duties sitting in your bank account before you can even consider making an offer.

Your monthly payments are also calculated by the number of years your mortgage is set for. The longer the amortization (25 to 30 years) the smaller your monthly payments will be, the shorter the term, (12 to 15 years) the heavier the monthly payments will be. For something that you will commit to for a minimum of 12 years, shouldn't you want to see if that is the best and most flexible arrangement you can find in the market?

Even a much more modest 280 / 217 (gross/saleable) square foot 1-bedroom flat in Sai Ying Pun is going for around HKD 5 million in the current market. For a property of this value, stamp duty is marginally lower at 2.25%, and if you are a PR and if this is your first property, you would also manage to get slightly better mortgage terms of 60% loan to value but still you will need over HKD$2 million for the down payment, stamp duties and solicitor fees.

Chapter Twelve:
Is it a good time to buy property?

Looking at the historical performance of property in Hong Kong, experts try to forecast whether it is the right time to buy, purely from a market standpoint.

According to the Hong Kong House Price Index, Hong Kong property has been very much a boom and bust market. In the decade to 1997, prices rose by 5x, and promptly collapsing by over a third in less than a year and then suffering a long and grueling bear market all the way to 2004, when they bottomed out at less than a third of their peak 1997 value.

Since then, and until mid-2015, property in Hong Kong followed China's ascent and rose by an incredible 4x, reaching prices 40% above previous 1997 peaks, with only occasional and moderate lulls – during the Global Financial

Crisis and SARS epidemic. That is over 15% per year purely in capital gains, without even factoring in rent.

The rising of house prices has not been any different to other markets. Like the Hong Kong market, both the Vancouver and London residential average property prices have seen a consistent rise in prices, much quicker than the rate of inflation.

According to Demographia, which compares house prices to incomes worldwide, those looking to buy property in Hong Kong face the least affordable market in the world by far, with an apartment costing 19 years of income as compared to Sydney at 12 and London and San-Francisco at 9.

UK Average House Prices – January 1991 to January 2015

Is it a good time to buy property?

Given the high prices and recent slowdown, some specialists have gone as far as to wager on a 20% fall over the coming years. That bubble has to pop one-way or another! Of course, Hong Kong property forecasters have been wrong more often then they are right.

And with Hong Kong still being a leading Asian business centre, and with the long-term demographics and growth rates of emerging Asian economies being more attractive than those of Europe, one can expect values to do better in the very long term, despite these near-term risks.

My advice is, "Don't try to time the market." The number one factor is your ability to afford a home without getting in over your head. That said, if you are looking for an edge, interest rates are near historic lows so now appears to be a better time than most for purchasing a home.

If you plan to resell in the future, don't buy the biggest and/or most expensive home on the block. These homes usually appreciate the least and present the biggest challenge when attempting to find a buyer. The smallest and/or least expensive home on the block often appreciates the most.

Inquire about your stamp duties, taxes, utility costs, management fees and government rents and rates so you are aware of the ongoing expenses. Look for units that the vendors are primed to sell, in any market you can find great deals.

That's why you need to have a real estate agent who you can trust and can present you with leads whenever they pop up. There is opportunity in both a bear market and a bull market. A real estate agent lives and breathes the property market everyday so if they are good, they can find great bargains in any market. When a unit is priced properly, or whether it is a distressed sale by the vendor, they will appear suddenly and be gone just as quickly in any market. Your task is to be ready when opportunity strikes because it will only strike when it is ready, it won't wait for you to be ready.

I'll wait for another black swan.

Chapter Thirteen
I'll wait for another black swan.

A black swan event is a metaphor that describes an event that comes as a surprise, has a major effect, and is often inappropriately rationalized after the fact with the benefit of hindsight. The term is based on an ancient saying, which presumed black swans did not exist, but the saying was rewritten after black swans were discovered in the wild.

A black swan is an event or occurrence that deviate beyond what is normally expected of a situation and is extremely difficult to predict; they are typically random and unexpected. Some psychologists suggest that extreme, rare events, which are unfamiliar, uncontrollable and potentially catastrophic, may be simply driven by fear because of uncertainty.

Examples of Past Black Swan Events

Asian Financial Crisis (1997)

In the last thirty years, the first black swan event was the Asian Financial Crisis. This was a period that gripped much of East Asia beginning in July 1997 and raised fears of a worldwide economic meltdown due to financial contagion.

The crisis started in Thailand with the financial collapse of the Thai baht after the Thai government was forced to float the baht due to lack of foreign currency to support its currency peg to the U.S. dollar. As the crisis spread, most of Southeast Asia and Japan saw slumping currencies, devalued stock markets and other asset prices, and a precipitous rise in private debt. Many Asian countries were affected by various degrees and all suffered from a loss of demand and confidence throughout the region.

Panic resulted among lenders, which led to a large withdrawal of credit from the crisis countries, causing a credit crunch and further bankruptcies. Governments raised domestic interest rates to exceedingly high levels to help diminish flight of capital and intervene in the exchange market by buying up any excess domestic currency at the fixed exchange rate with foreign reserves.

I'll wait for another black swan.

Another possible cause of the sudden risk shock in Hong Kong may also be attributable to its handover of sovereignty back to China on 1st of July 1997. During the 1990s, hot money flew into the Southeast Asia region through financial hubs, especially Hong Kong. The investors were often ignorant of the actual fundamentals or risk profiles of the respective economies, and once the crisis gripped the region, coupled with the political uncertainty regarding the future of Hong Kong as an Asian financial centre led some investors to withdraw from Asia altogether. This shrink in investments only worsened the financial conditions in Asia.

With uncertainty and unrest, in 1998 there was a property price collapse; from 1997 to 2003 Hong Kong residential property prices fell by 61% and overnight interest rates skyrocketed to 280% and unemployment soared, lending shuddered to a halt and inflation morphed to deflation.

SARS Epidemic (2002 -2004)

Asia still had not recovered from the crisis when SARS (Severe Acute Respiratory Syndrome) began its wave through Southeast Asia. It caused the worst economic crisis ever with a wave of bank failures and currency devaluations that swept through the region. The economies of Hong Kong, Singapore and Taiwan had not just abruptly stopped growing but shrank, the economies of Malaysia and Thailand and even China's booming industrial expansion came to a standstill.

With nervous customers staying away from stores and restaurants in areas where cases have been reported, and travellers cancelling or postponing trips, industries that offer services to people, like restaurants, hotels, airlines or cinemas, were hit particularly hard. Industries that involved discretionary products such as luxury goods were also heavily affected.

Research from Princeton University in 2004, published a paper concluded that during the epidemic, housing prices fell by 8% and transaction volume decreased by about 30% compared to the same period in 2002. By the end of 2002, Hong Kong residential housing prices had declined by more than 65% from their peak level in 1997.

Transaction volume in the housing market decreased because of the rise in search cost. The SARS epidemic involved unknown risks and caused a great deal of unrest and anxiety across Hong Kong society. Because of the way outbreaks occurred, some buildings were thought to be more susceptible to SARS than others due to their characteristics.

I'll wait for another black swan.

It appeared that potential buyers were deterred from

HK Secondary Residential Housing Prices

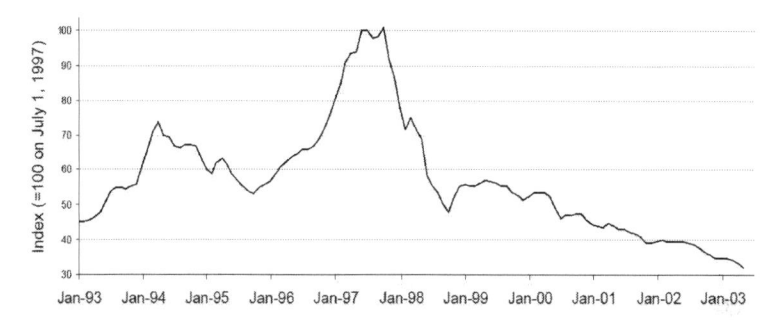

their usual house searching activities by the increase in search costs due to the risk of contracting SARS during the epidemic. Because people chose to stay in their homes in fear of the possibility of contracting the virus, virtually no one was shopping for property during this period.

Weekly Price Movements in the first 26 weeks of 2003

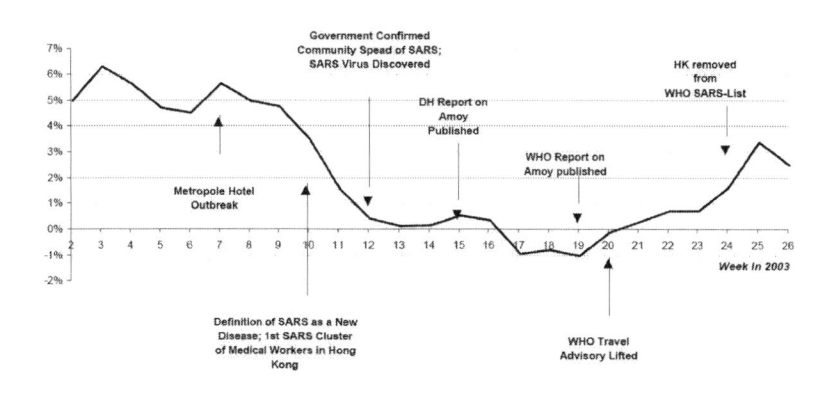

Global Financial Crisis (2008)

Slowly after Hong Kong recovered from the SARS epidemic, came the onset of the Global Financial Crisis of 2008 where many countries viewed it as a purely American subprime mortgage problem. Yet, the crisis rapidly developed and spread into a global economic shock.

This resulted in the US government bailing out several large financial institutions, such as AIG, Fannie Mae, and Freddie Mac. In addition, coupled with the trouble in America, a number of European banks failed and stock markets declined across the board. Many Asian countries, far from the epicenter of the financial troubles, were relatively safe at the beginning.

Ever since 1997, China has been Hong Kong's largest trading partner, accounting for about half of Hong Kong's exports by value. Hong Kong has since moved its manufacturing industry to China, its service industry has grown rapidly and accounted for more than 90% of the territory's GDP in 2009.

Heavily dependent on trading, Hong Kong was hit hard by the Global Financial crisis in terms of exports, GDP, and employment. Impacted by the crisis, economic growth dropped from 6.4% in 2007 to 2.5% in 2008, and then to further negative growth of -2.5% in the last quarter of 2009. Total

I'll wait for another black swan.

exports dropped by 21.8%, the stock market saw a sharp decline with the Hang Seng Index plunging 48% from a year before.

However, by this time, the government response greatly improved and was swift to react. By putting forward a series of measure, they were able to counter balance the impact, stabilize the financial market, support enterprise, and create employment. Externally, China's central government also announced measures to boost Hong Kong's economy through cross-boundary infrastructure projects.

With a service economy, Hong Kong's financial sector was hard hit by the crisis as output and employment declined. Fortunately, by this time, most banks in Hong Kong were sufficiently capitalized and had raised their provision levels so they were able to weather the crisis.

In addition, Hong Kong's sound banking system, minimal public debt, strong legal system, ample foreign exchange reserves, rigorous anticorruption measures, and close ties with China, enabled it to quickly respond to the financial crisis.

While Hong Kong's open economy left it exposed to the global economic slowdown, its increasing integration with China has mitigated the effect of the financial crisis. Trade, tourism, and financial links between the two economies helped Hong Kong recover quicker than many outside observers anticipated.

Particularly, foreign investors continued to contribute capital in flows as they took advantage of Hong Kong's "free" market economy with high accessibility to the China mainland economy. Although Hong Kong's GDP fell in 2009 as a result of the Global Financial Crisis, a recovery began in the third quarter 2009, and the economy grew nearly 6.8% in 2010.

The Next Black Swan (??)

Of course, one man's black swan event might be another man's "I told you so". Will another financial crisis happen in the next thirty years moving forward? Will investors, lenders, and borrowers be as overleveraged as they were in 1997 or have there been measures implemented to prevent that from happening again?

The chance that another Asian country will make some sort of financial mistake and cause their currency to devalue within days may or may not happen again. What are the chances that there will be another sub-prime mortgage crisis in America that all the homeowners will again default on their mortgages?

I'll wait for another black swan.

Would there be better precaution any virus or sickness now that a country has taken measures to address this type of threat?

Hong Kong has taken the lessons to heart, both in its approach to managing new diseases and maintaining hygiene. All these years after the outbreak, apartment and office blocks still boast of how many times daily they sanitise lift buttons, hand rails, door knobs and almost all public surfaces. Masks are de rigueur if you have a cold, and a sneezing or coughing fit on public transport meets with disapproving glances.

After each successive black swan event, Hong Kong appears to have recovered better every time. Even if there were another major catastrophe, everyone now would be more ready or better prepared for another financial melt down to happen. When it happens again, and you anticipate property prices to plummet, how quickly will you be able to react? How ready can you be?

When financial hardships hits, banks usually become more conservative in their lending. Interest rates will be higher and lending criteria will be more stringent. Property prices will stagnate and decrease. If you see prices fall, how far do you think the prices will drop? At what point do you feel that it is time for you to buy in? If you were not already holding cash, chances are by the time you see an opportunity, you may not be able to move quickly enough to borrow or leverage as well as when the market was good.

During a market crisis you also need to be less picky in what you are buying because the overriding criteria when picking your investment is the timing and not the property. You cannot be too picky in what you buy during a crisis.

Black swan events happen when you are not ready for the unknown unknowns. They are entirely unpredictable so when people say that they plan on waiting for the next one, when it happens, there is a strong chance that they may not be as prepared as they want to be.

During the subprime lending crisis in America, the known unknowns the banks were prepared for was that some homeowners may possibly default on their loans. What they did not anticipate were the unknown unknowns – that all homeowners would default on their loans. The day when Lehman Brothers announced their closing in 2008, the HSBC stock price dropped from around 192 to the low 30s in a matter of days and till this day, it has never fully recovered. At the same time, property prices also dropped but it was a mere dip in the

I'll wait for another black swan.

pool and in a matter of a few months the prices quickly bounced back without a blemish.

Herd Mentality

Also I need to talk about herd mentality. You say that you will be ready when the next financial tsunami hits, but when everything is tumbling down and people you know are losing their jobs because of drastic company cuts, would you be so bold to jump in and drop a few million Hong Kong dollars on a property not knowing whether in a few more weeks, the property could fall another few thousand dollars? When will the prices hit bottom?

It takes great nerve to jump into the property market during a volatile market. It takes even greater nerve to do the exact opposite of what everyone else is doing when all around you the markets are falling and people are trying to salvage whatever they have left. Can you be so bold as to say that this is the perfect time to invest and buy when everyone else is running away? People can say with confidence after a crisis has bounced back what they should have done but how many people can say that they could actually take the plunge when it happens? You cannot use a black swan event as the barometer to tell you when you are ready to buy.

Chapter Fourteen
The Secret to Your Success

As you know I am biased towards the countries I have invested in myself. But I have reasons to buy where I have bought. In Hong Kong and in London, there is the mentality that land ownership is important and everyone should aspire to one day own his or her first home.

You would prefer to buy where individuals can purchase freehold land. Freehold ownership means permanent and absolute tenure of the land or property with freedom to dispose of it at will.

With the mentality of wanting to buy freehold property in the UK and Canada, the property market is very robust, bringing with it a strong secondary market because people want to live in these countries. With the desire to move to these countries to start a better life and to have more opportunities, there is economic diversification.

This is a strong lure for many people to come to these countries to live, to work and grow. These countries are not just vacation countries where the only strong economy that keeps the economy alive is tourism and foreign investments; these countries have a thriving economy, strong currency and healthy foreign trade with other countries.

When you buy in these countries, you can also look at who is buying and why. Primarily it is best to ask what is the owner-occupier ratio of these units. With units that have 80% owner-occupier ratio, that leaves only 20% of units in a building that are available for lease.

This creates competition for tenantable units so applicants compete for them and owners have the choice to choose among applicants. If there are more non-owner-occupied units available there may be more available stock for applicants to choose from. With more stock, landlords compete for tenants so prices soften or if there are not enough tenants to move into vacant homes, you end up with ghost towns where areas of the city have hundreds of units with very low occupancy rate.

So Why Buy Leasehold in Hong Kong Property?

Unlike the countries of the UK and Canada, Hong Kong property ownership is only leasehold. A leasehold estate is an ownership of a temporary right to hold land or property in which a lessee or a tenant holds rights of real property by some form of title from a lessor or landlord. The landlord in Hong Kong is the Hong Kong government with the exception of the indigenous people of Hong Kong who hold freehold property.

So, if you are not allowed to own freehold property, why would you still consider investing in Hong Kong property? Well…in the Global Financial Centres Index which is compiled semi-annually by the London-based British think-tank Z/Yen, Hong Kong ranks fourth behind London, New York City and Singapore in the top global financial centres around the world. For a tiny city, it has a lot of weight on its financial shoulders.

It is the home to the highest concentration of banking institutions in the world with over 71 of the largest 100 international banks having operations in the territory. It also supports the largest concentration of fund managers in Asia with more than 290 fund management companies in operation there.

For more than a century, Hong Kong has served as the gateway to mainland China and has the necessary expertise, information and facilities to tap into the Chinese marketplace, which has made Hong Kong the largest trading partner of mainland China. The country's high living standards, quality of life and environment are frequently ranked among the most attractive in Asia for foreign-skilled professionals.

Hong Kong has a strong, efficient and transparent legal and judicial framework, based on common English law, which presents a favorable regulatory and business environment with a high degree of banking confidentiality. It also has a favorable tax regime, with no tax on foreign-sourced income remitted to Hong Kong, no capital gains tax, no withholding tax in dividends and no interest and inheritance tax or VAT.

With extremely favourable conditions to invest and strong reasons to come to Hong Kong to live, there is still enormous draw for investors, business oriented individuals, entrepreneurs and businesses to buy and live in this incredible city.

If you are a permanent resident of Hong Kong, both from a legal standpoint and in practice, then you need to have a home, have an investment horizon of many years, are not subject to punitive stamp duties and have access to reasonable mortgage financing. In this situation, buying Hong Kong property could make sense for you. With rental yields at around 3%, and without much room for further appreciation, that is the sort of return you could reasonably expect from your investment.

On the other hand, if you have an international perspective and are thinking whether to buy property in Hong Kong purely from an investment standpoint, it might make sense to consider other prime markets. Most have lower stamp duty, require lower mortgage deposits, are at more affordable price levels and are linked to less volatile economies.

If you still want to consider Hong Kong property, keep in mind that you should be buying to hold for the long term. With all the stamp duties in place, the Hong Kong market is not for the speculative investor. The stamp duties are in place to stop the "hard core property flippers", those who buy a unit in the morning and by the evening have sold it off for a HKD $2,000,000.00 gain. Because Hong Kong has no capital gains tax, this used to be a possibility for individuals.

Unlike other cities where there is always the possibility of city expansion and growth, there is limited land in Hong Kong for developers to build. With the Chinese border north of Hong Kong, there is no more available land to expand its territory. The only way developers can increase the available square footage of property to build is to bring down older low-level buildings and build higher blocks. By doing this, they increase the number of units from 30 units to possible over a 150+.

You want to buy where there is a land scarcity and where stock is scarce. Tenants will compete for units as well as landlords when buying. Hong Kong is the perfect example of a city with limited stock. There is a limited amount of land developers that can build first hand property. In respects to second hand property, it is still in high demand. The chances you will be able to turn a profit on its capital growth in 3 to 5 years or just have a good high yield return in your rental income is strong.

(For more in depth explanation, go to http://michelle-cheng.com)

Is it the right time to buy?

When people ask me this question, I don't think they are asking whether now is a good time to buy so they can sell in a year and make a huge profit.
I think what they are really asking is, does it make sense for me, in my current situation, to buy a home. That's a tougher question to answer broadly because everyone's specific situation

is different and can vary based on a variety of factors, but let's try to break it down.

How Long Will You Stay?

One of the most important factors to take into account is your estimated time horizon. That is, how long do you plan to live or own the home? Elements such as job security, changing careers, or pursuing an advanced degree can have a big influence on this.

Your time frame matters because there are a fair amount of "frictional costs" involved when buying and selling real estate. A longer time horizon gives you more of an opportunity to realize price appreciation on the home, to offset any transactional costs.

When you are considering whether you should buy or rent, one of the most important factors is how long do you plan to live in the area. It may make sense to rent if their time horizon is five years or less since they'll have to pay closing costs and agent fees twice through the process. Each situation and area is different, so you need to run the numbers to determine what makes sense.

I have gone through my story to tell you how much success I have had in my property investments. There is no magic involved in this process. It did involve a lot of hard work and determination on my part but there are a handful of significant factors that I keep in mind when deciding when to jump on the next opportunity.

In this book, I've gone through what things to avoid for a new investor and what things you need to consider when investing in property. So why am I going to the trouble of sharing this information with you?

Again, it is to speed up your progress or reassure your decisions when you make your steps into property investment. I was fortunate to have the right people around me to guide me in my decision and now I am here to guide you.

I tell you this because there is a secret that most gurus will not share with you and it is something that has to be mentioned because again, knowing this WILL SPEED UP your progress.

THE SECRET is that the great deals come up when they are ready, not when you are ready. The great deals come in the size and shape they want not what you want. The great deals come in prices and values at what they want not what you want.

In other words your property investment could be available tomorrow or six months from now...you never know which. **The important thing <u>is to always be ready to take advantage</u> of a great investment when the opportunity comes up...because it will.**

Do You Have The Money?

Equally important is whether you have sufficient upfront and ongoing funds to pay for a place you would want to live in. Upfront costs include the down payment and closing costs which includes solicitor fees, agent fees and stamp duties, but money should also be set aside for an emergency fund or post-transaction cash that may go towards renovation costs and repairs.

On an ongoing basis, you'll need to know if your salary is enough to comfortably pay a mortgage, homeowners insurance, any management fees that the building will ask for and government rates and taxes. Financial planners like to see ongoing housing costs less than 28% of gross income and total debt less than 36% of gross income.

Don't stress about figuring out these answers alone though. A quick call to a mortgage broker or lender can give you a good understanding of whether you have enough upfront and ongoing money to buy a home. If it turns out you don't have sufficient funds currently, meeting with a financial planner could help you put a plan in place to save enough money for a future purchase.

So What is The Answer?

Determining when the best time for *you* to buy may be much more important than deciding whether home prices are "on sale." None of us can time the market, but we can time our needs.

Be sure to review your specific situation with subject matter experts to see if you are well positioned to buy a home. Once you're ready, you can work with your real estate agent to look at local market trends and data, such as months of inventory, days on market, and asking vs. closing prices to see if your market is tilting in favour of buyers or sellers.

So many times, I've heard many people tell me that they "feel" that the property market is too high right now so they are going to wait until the market softens before they go in. Or that they saw a place that they really liked but they did not go through the pre-approval process of applying for a loan and by the time they had submitted all their paperwork, the unit was sold.

When I suspect an opportunity I don't usually go by "feel" alone, like property investors, their favourite mantra is still **"location, location, location"** however, location is actually more than just the address. Location has a few considerations:-

Development

The prices can differ enormously within and across neighbourhoods, suburbs, and districts. Access to transportation, schools, shopping centres, and jobs all influence property prices. It is the proximity to what people care about that is a driving factor to how much a property is worth.

The Potential for Gentrification

Location really matters when you can predict gentrification. Typically you will find these locations right on the outskirts of the already in-demand neighbourhoods, with old housing stock & low home ownership rates. With time, these factors will create attractive opportunities for developers which create the demand for gentrification to unfold creating the possibility of a strong secondary market which you will gain access to when you are ready to sell.

Strong Secondary Market

It is important to have a strong secondary market. The first homebuyer is the primary buyer. When the primary buyer decides to sell the home, it becomes a secondary market asset. Imagine what would happen to the housing market if homes could not enter a secondary market. Housing prices would be far less flexible and accurate than they are today, and almost no homebuyers would enter the primary market, either. There is not much incentive to buy a permanently large asset that is locked into a specific location. If there is no secondary market, property purchasing would not be considered an investment if you cannot gain on any capital growth. If there is not a strong secondary market, it would make it very difficult for you to sell your property at the time when you're ready to sell. Most of the Hong Kong property stock is largely secondary and also very limited so buyers bid for property whenever they come on the market keeping the secondary alive and very active. Even though the Hong Kong property is only sold as leasehold, there still is a high demand for leasehold ownership.

Owner-Occupier Ratio

The higher the owner occupancy level in a complex the higher the appeal. If more owners want to buy to live in these complexes it means that there is some appeal to live in that particular area. Economic development of that area will rise creating more draw to the neighbourhood. This creates appeal. Tenants will compete for the few units that are not owner occupied.

You do not want to be purchasing in areas where the owner occupancy ratio is low because if there are too many investors buying up the units, there will be too many available units to let and quite possibly not enough tenants. For large developments where many or only investors are buying in an area, you may end up with many unoccupied units in a complex creating a ghost town-like feeling in a building where in the evenings there are hardly any lights on in the builidng.

All these points that you need to keep in mind when you are looking for investment property may seem daunting but the more you look at property the easier it is to see whether this investment is a good one to make.

Chapter Fifteen
The Six Steps to Buying Property

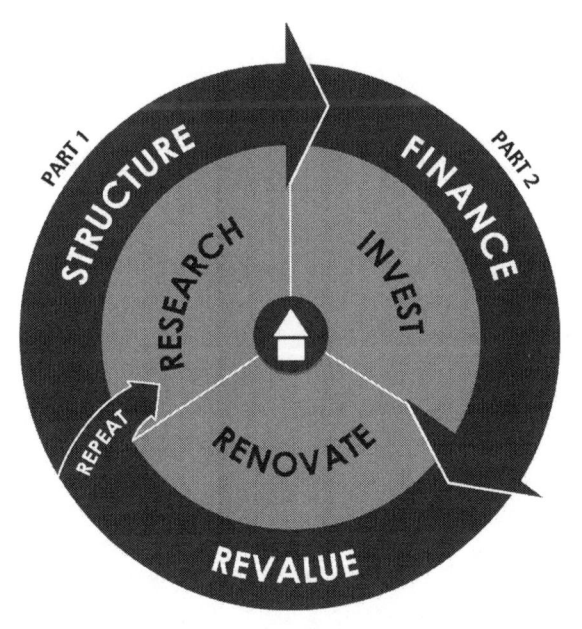

PART 1 STRUCTURE
PART 2 FINANCE — INVEST
PART 3 RESEARCH · RENOVATE · REVALUE · REPEAT

From making the initial decision that you want to buy property, you need to do your research to make sure you are fully informed in your investment decision. You want to ensure that you are making a profitable investment that will be a real financial asset for you now and into the future.

There are six simple steps to consider when you decide to go into the market to buy property. Now I advise that you may need to move back and forth around this paradigm and there are steps you will spend more time on before you move ahead to the next. What is more important is that you consider all the steps before you decide to take the plunge into purchasing.

Step 1: Research

It is best to start your search is with a fairly clear picture of what you want. Do you want a one bedroom, two bedrooms or three, an apartment or even a house? Do you want it smack dab in the busiest area of SOHO where you can literally crawl straight home from the bar or would you want somewhere slightly farther from the evening crowds but still easily accessible to public transportation. Do you own a car and therefore need to have parking accessibility? For most people in Hong Kong, do you have hired helped that you need to have a maid's room for?

You should understand the neighborhood the property you are looking for is situated in. In Hong Kong, which district do you think you will find a high occupancy rate with a good yield? By looking at the demographics, you can estimate the average age of residents, composition of families and even their education, occupation and possibly financial level who would live in a particular area. The demographics in Hong Kong are less diverse and you tend to get more educated individuals who can afford to rent in the more busier places in Central Hong Kong.

Before you purchase an investment property look at what you could get if you were to rent it out. You may plan on living there for a few years but maybe in the future something may change. Perhaps, you get married and want to start a family, you may need to find something larger so you decide to rent out your place instead. Rental prices can fluctuate neighbourhood to neighbourhood, so it is also a good idea to have a look at the average rental income in the area in respect to the size of place you are to buy and where you want to buy. With rentals, you also need to understand whether the area that you will be buying has a strong occupancy rate. Are most of the units tenanted or owner occupied? How quickly can you rent out the unit once the last tenant vacates the premises? What type of tenants will most likely want to live there and for how long?

When looking at the property market in Hong Kong, where would you want to buy to be assured that your property will have a higher chance of occupancy?

Tourists and visitors come to the city to experience the vibrancy of this densely populated urban centre of Hong Kong. It is a major port and global financial hub with a skyscraper-studded skyline. Business people who have business in the city would prefer to stay in and around Central and/or around the west of Hong Kong island. If you are looking at creating a unit for short term leasing, you want to focus on the areas where there is quick and easy transportation access and located right in the middle of town.

With the majority of the population taking public transportation daily, Hong Kong has a highly developed transportation network so properties that have quick access to these vital transportation arteries of the city are highly desired by any type of investor. Many individuals who have lived in Hong Kong for a number of years do still prefer to stay on the Hong Kong side of the island rather than moving across the water to Kowloon. So areas where there is a lot of interest in investment properties like the west side of Hong Kong may require extra capital, so it is best to be informed of all the steps before you submit your offer.

However, perhaps you are looking for a home away from the hustle and bustle of the city. There are many outlying islands around the main island that provide a beach-like resort feel. If that is what you want to choose, there is nothing stopping you from making that purchase but keep in mind that if you later on want to sell your place off, the next buyer will hopefully be looking for the same thing.

Step 2: Structure

Having the right structure will help ensure that you protect your investment while saving on tax and avoid stamp duty penalties at the same time. Once you decide to buy an investment property you should decide what type of vehicle you would like to use in order to create an investment that works most to your advantage. You need to obtain professional advice from a lawyer, an accountant or a wealth management professional in whose name the property is to be bought.

Individual - Owning an investment property in an individual's own name is by far the simplest and cheapest option. Despite the lack of asset protection, any negative gearing losses generated from the property may offset the income of the individual, which will be particularly attractive to high income earners. Borrowing equity if a house is under personal title can be clearer but you become very transparent as to the number of assests you own.

In Hong Kong, there is no capital gains tax so when you sell your property you are not taxed on the profit; however, in other countries such as Canada, Australia and the United Kingdom the percentage of capital gains tax that is charged can be quite high so you may want to consider sheltering your properties to pay less tax. If you were transferring property from one individual to the next, you can also be charged stamp duties in Hong Kong to change titles so there are both benefits and shortcomings to holding property under individual title for residential property in Hong Kong.

Company - A company is a separate legal entity at law. Accordingly, if an individual sets up a company to buy an investment property, the individual does not own the property, so if the individual gets sued, the property will not be exposed to risk as it legally belongs to the company. However, whoever owns the shares in the company indirectly owns all of the assets of the company. Therefore, if an at-risk individual owns all the shares in the company, which in turn owns the investment property, the structure may not provide the intended asset protection feature.

Any net rental income derived by the company will be taxed at the corporate tax rate. At this point in the discussion, it is best that you speak to a tax professional to get all the information involved with profit declaration of your company.

In Hong Kong, when transferring title from one person to another, having a property owned under a company structure is subject to a lesser stamp duty than transferring between two individuals. By selling the shares of the company – a non-trading company that strictly owns one residential property, you pay only for the cost of transferring shares of a company and not the stamp duty for the sale of a residential property.

However, if you decide to open a company for the purpose of buying a residential property, you will pay a 30% stamp duty based on the sale price of the residential property because it is a company that is buying a property and not an individual with permanent residency status. This is stamp duty has been created as a possible cooling measure to slow down rising property market in Hong Kong.

Trust - At law, a trust is a relationship under which the trustee looks after the trust's assets for the benefit of the beneficiaries. If it is set up properly, a discretionary trust may offer reasonably effective asset protection as the beneficiaries of the trust are generally not presently entitled to the income and/or capital of the trust until the trustee makes a resolution to distribute the income and/or capital.

For taxation purposes, a discretionary trust provides maximum flexibility in terms of the annual net rental income of the trust as the trustee has the discretion to distribute different amounts of income to different beneficiaries, with regards to the respective tax position of each beneficiary from year to year.

Summary

Having the right structure for your investment property needs to be one of the first steps you take before you actually put the down payment on the property you wish to buy. I made that mistake when I purchased my last property in Hong Kong. My brother wanted me to invest in a unit together so we purchased it under joint ownership. That was an incredible mistake for me. Under joint ownership any decision made would require both individuals to agree.

There is a greater problem now with Hong Kong. When the Hong Kong government changed its stamp duty policies on the 4th of November, 2016. It raised its stamp duties to 15% for individuals who were buying additional residential properties if they already owned one in Hong Kong. Originally if you wanted to buy a HKD $6 million unit, the stamp duty percentage is 6% or $360,000.00. Now with the rise to 15%, the stamp duty is now $900,000.00.

This stamp duty has greatly affected smaller units because it has eliminated many investors who were just looking to buy for investment only. With the unit, half under my name, I am now tied to this unit and have no flexibilty to borrow or sell without getting my brother involved. Most investors are no longer looking at buying small units because with the heavy stamp duty, there is no yield now to invest.

What I should have done initially was to open a company and have the company buy the unit with my brother and myself as the directors. With the company owning the unit, it would have still allowed me movement around this joint ownership. However, going that route now is also virtually impossible now because after November 4, 2016, if a company buys residential property they will now pay 30% stamp duty.

If I were to transfer ownership from joint to single and even if the person taking over the title is one of the joint parties, the government will still recognize it as a sale and will charge the regular 15% stamp duty. Basically now, I am no longer sure I will ever be able to sell this property. There are no buyers who would want to buy to live there themselves and the stamp duty is too expensive for investors to consider. The only thing for me now is to just hold on to the unit and let it run as a rental unit until another solution presents itself in the future.

So not all the decisions I have made have gone as smoothly as I hoped so I advise you now to think about how you want to structure your ownership before you are past the point of it being too late to change it.

Step 3: Invest – Once you have a general idea of where you would like to buy your property, you need to figure out how much you can borrow to buy your investment property. If you are a resident of countries like Canada, Australia and the UK, the general rule when you purchase a residential property is that the down payment required can be as little as a 5 to 10% deposit.

However, because of many attempts by the Hong Kong government to implement cooling measures to slow down the housing market, the minimum down payment required by all the banks for units is 50%. Any unit that costs HK$10 million or above, the loan-to-value (LTV) ratio is 50% and as a general rule any unit between HKD$6 million to $10 million, the loan-to-value ratio is 60%.

Any unit that costs less than HKD$6 million will have greater flexibility in lending. For new developments, developers in Hong Kong have in the past offered to finance the large portion of the difference to help the buyer borrow up to as much as 95% of the purchase price. There are other conditions that may apply when evaluation your borrowing capability.

You also need to consider the age and condition of the building. There are various types of residential buildings in Hong Kong. One type of building of interest for some is the old Hong Kong walk-up. These buildings are usually three to five stories and do not have an elevator hence the term "walk-up". These buildings tend to be older with many reaching and passing the age of 50.

Some banks when considering older buildings such as Hong Kong walk ups, may only offer 40-50% lending while others would not even consider lending at all.

There are rare opportunities that you would buy first hand properties. With first hand properties, the developers usually offers discounts and greater lending flexibility to the buyer but the cost per square foot is usually fixed so there is less flexibility in regards to the negotiated price. In Hong Kong, the demand for first hand property sales has risen even greater than the time I bought my first unit.

Now whenever there is a new development launch, in order to buy property you need to enter into a lottery system. You present your 5% deposit cheque and your ballot goes into the draw. Only if your ballot is drawn do you get a swing of the bat to purchase a unit in the development and again, you are given little choice as to which floor your unit will be.

(For more information on the entire cost for your property purchase, go to http://michelle-cheng.com)

Step 4: Finance – All mortgages work in the same basic way: you borrow money to buy a property, pay interest on the loan and eventually pay it back. Then they start getting complicated and you are looking at:

- Different interest rates
- Different ways to repay
- Borrowing for different periods of time
- Particular mortgages for special situations
- Various charges to pay

Repayment mortgages – This is the basic way of repaying all mortgages. With repayment mortgages, each month, you repay some of the interest you owe plus some of the principal you have borrowed. Usually at the beginning of the loan, the percentage you pay towards the interest is more than you pay towards the principal, only when you get to the end of your mortgage do your payments go more towards the principal. Usually by the end of the mortgage period, often 25 years, you will have paid back everything you owe and you will own your home outright.

Interest only mortgages – With interest-only loans, you pay just the interest month by month and repay the capital at the end of the period with money you have saved elsewhere.

This is quite different from the repayment mortgage because at the end of the loan you will have to find enough money to repay the whole debt. Usually principal and interest loans help you budget your monthly payments so through time, your loan will get smaller. With an interest only mortgage, you must be confident of having the money on hand when the time comes to repay. If you don't, you might have to sell the house to pay off the mortgage.

You could be lucky and find that your home has increased so much in price that the extra value is enough to remortgage and pay off the debt.

The big advantage of interest only mortgages is that your monthly repayments are lower than with any other mortgage because you are paying only the interest due. This is a great way for buyers who want the lowest monthly repayments and are confident they will have enough money to repay the debt at the end of the mortgage.

Fixed rate mortgages – Fixed rate mortgages are popular, particularly with first time buyers, because your mortgage rate is fixed for a set number of years – usually 2, 3 or 5 years but sometimes 10 years. You know exactly how much you will be paying each month for that length of time, regardless of what happens to the interest.

The downside is that you will be stuck on a higher rate if other mortgage rates go down. You can get out of a fixed rate mortgage but there will be an early repayment charge to pay for switching before the end of the period.

When the mortgage comes to an end, you will be put on the lender's standard variable rate (SVR) which will probably have a higher interest rate than you have been paying. In that case you can apply for another fixed rate deal.

This mortgage is good for buyers who are budgeting carefully and want to know exactly how much they will be paying over the next few years.

Tracker mortgage – Tracker mortgages move in line (i.e. they track) with a nominated interest rate, which is usually governed by the Hong Kong Monetary Authority. The actual mortgage rate you pay will be a set interest rate above or below the base rate. When base rate goes up, your mortgage rate will go up by the same amount. When the base rate comes down, your rate will come down.

Some lenders set a minimum rate below which your interest rate will never drop but there is no limit to how high it can go. With base rates at 0.5% and an add-on rate of 1.5%, your mortgage rate will be 2%. This type of mortgage is the typical Hong Kong mortgage that most banks give out.

Summary – There are many other types of mortgages – buy-to-let mortgages, first time buyer mortgages, offset mortgage and capped rate mortgages, etc. Many of these are not available in Hong Kong but can be in other countries you may consider investing in. There is a lot to take into account before deciding which mortgage you want. You will find it helps if you have a broad understanding of how mortgages work and the various different kinds of mortgages available.

Step 5: Renovate – The nicer your property, the longer you will likely keep your tenants. With that in mind, these improvements should make your property desirable without putting too much strain on your wallet.

Treat it as a House, not a Home - Firstly, it is important not to work along the same stringent standards you may apply to your own home. As sad as this may sound, there is no point in over-renovating a property, or striving for "picture perfect" standards because your tenants are not going to treat it with the same care as they would their own property. To them, it is only a temporary home and they will treat it that way. The most important goal is to make sure the property looks inviting and liveable. Try not to get emotionally involved or you will overcapitalize on your property

Give Tenants a Vision – When a potential tenant tours the property, they are asking themselves a very important question: "Can I see myself living here?" You need to confront this head-on by presenting the property in the best possible light (*pun intended*).

For example, if the property looks dingy and dusty, then clean it. If it looks dark, open all the blinds, turn on all the lights, or paint the walls a light color. Perhaps, you should buy additional floor lamps for extra lighting. If the property seems small, consider knocking down a wall to create a more open feeling. In Hong Kong, most units will be considered relatively small so you will need a bit more creativity to see how you can maximize the space that you have.

If the property seems desolate and vacant, consider staging the unit with furniture. However, since moving furniture and finding storage to keep furniture is not as easy in

Hong Kong as it is in other countries, you may consider just keeping the unit with as little furniture as possible.

Many people in Hong Kong tend to install built-in furniture. Built-in wardrobes may come in handy but keep the built-in furniture to a minimal. I have seen units that have everything built-in including the desks and beds. A landlord may feel that a double bed frame may be big enough for their tenant but when a client is over six foot tall, they will ask if there is anyway the bed can be taken out so he can bring in his own.

The humidity in Hong Kong is also a killer for furniture and electrical work. I have seen homes with built in cabinetry, beds and wardrobes. I have seen electricity work done so with just the push of the button everything slide up and down and lights turn on and off. However, in just a matter of a few years, electrical wiring and parts starts to rust and breakdown, and the woodwork starts to look old and weathered. Your initial investment towards customized furniture has been diminished because of the work of Grandfather Time and Mother Nature.

Sometimes assisting the tenants with a vision will require some imagination but keep your renovations to the basics.

Repair before Replacing – The problem a lot of landlords face in this regard, is that they will rush in, clear out the contents, paint the entire interior, lay down new flooring in hopes to usher in new tenants as quickly as possible. While this sounds quite sensible, bear in mind that this is expensive and rarely does the entire place needed to be overhauled.

- **Flooring** – Due to the level of dust that can accumulate in Hong Kong, I personally avoid carpeting all together. Tenants can always purchase their own rugs to warm up the place. You can opt to use wood laminate flooring, which looks great and is tough as nails while being less expensive than hardwoods. An even better option is to change to tiles. They are extremely durable and now you can get tiles that look like wood paneling. In case of any plumbing issues, you would not be worried that water will damage your flooring.
- **Ceilings** – Ceilings rarely need to be painted. Unless the tenants/previous occupants were heavy smokers or extremely messy cooks, the ceiling will probably look clean.
- **Walls** - New paint in a lighter shade is always nice. You can use a flat or semi-gloss finish for walls. Whatever color you choose, make it a lighter color and paint the whole house the same shade, except ceilings, which should be white. Walls

should be painted every 5 years. A fresh coat of light-colored paint will make your property look brand-new.

- Maintenance Issues – Regular servicing of your air conditioning units will extend the life of your units. Water valves, supply line hoses, washing machine and dishwasher hoses and drains pose the biggest leak and flood risk.
- **Buy and replace fixtures** – Examples of fixtures that need replacing are:
    - Door handles that stick
    - Toilets that constantly run
    - Lighting older than 20 years old that look dreadfully outdated
    - Cabinet hardware that has lost its finish
    - Mini-blinds with missing slats
    - Faucets or tubs that drip

These inexpensive fixes will help update the property, appeal to potential tenants, and reduce after-the-fact maintenance.

Focus on the Kitchen and Bathrooms - Kitchens and bathrooms usually provide the greatest "wow" factor. Tenants, like everyone else, do not want to be washing themselves in a dirty or moldy bathroom. They also don't want to cook in an outdated kitchen from the 1970s. If you are going to upgrade any specific rooms in the property, I would start with these two.

Summary

Be methodical when surveying the entire property. Try to view the property turnover as lots of little jobs, not one big job. If the little jobs are not entirely necessary, then leave them for next time.

You should strive to deliver a quality property when the tenant moves-in, but very few residents will ever notice all the extra care you took in your preparation.

Upon moving in, I provide my tenants with an Inventory and Condition Checklist, which gives them the opportunity to note any repair or defect within the property. If possible, I repair or remedy everything they mention and then note the repair date on the document.

Despite what decorators will tell you, a good minded tenant does not really want to live in a super-plush, sleek overly styled property, but rather a functional living space where they will feel comfortable and will enjoy spending their time. Sometimes your decorating taste may not be the same as the tenants, so do not personalize your unit too much. Allow them to see it for themselves as a home they want to live in. I do get the occasional client who is looking for a lease and their request list is that they want everything brand new with fresh coat of paint, new flooring and beautiful from a new balcony. I can definitely find them something of this level but I tell them that if the landlord has this unit that has a great view and the unit is in great shape, be prepared to pay their price.

One major detail that may only be susceptible to Hong Kong property is that when banks value property they base their decisions on recent transactions in the building and how much they are willing to lend money based on the current property markets. That means that banks do not consider the interior condition of the unit to add any additional value to the price of the unit.

Therefore, if you spend a large amount of money renovating your place, that amount will not reflect a higher valuation. The only thing renovations will raise is the desirability of your unit and therefore tenants can rent it out sooner. It will ensure the happiness of your tenants renting the place and lower your maintenance requests and possibly increase your rental income.

As an investor you should realize that you might not necessarily recover the total cost of these improvements if you decide to sell in the near future. Keep all things to a necessary minimum and never overcapitalize on your investment.

Step 6: Revalue – You need to re-evaluate your financial properties to analyse your property's performance. A market comparison is more than necessary in aiding you to establish how far you should go with renovations and repairs so that you steer clear of overcapitalization while boosting your financial returns. On that note, it is sensible to compare your property's conditions and rent against those of similar properties on the market. This way, you can estimate approximate running costs and decide whether there is a need to enhance the property or not.

The other point to look at is whether you have made a good investment when you first bought the property. Depending on how long you have owned your property, there are three options you can consider:
1. SELL: If the present value of the property has risen to a greater value than maintaining and managing it as a rental property, you could sell your current property,

pulling out your net equity and buy another. In some countries, the problem with selling is you have to pay capital gains tax. There is no capital gains tax in Hong Kong but if you sell your property within 36 months of purchasing it, you will pay Seller Stamp duties.

2. REFINANCE: If you don't want to sell it, you could refinance your current property and use the loan proceeds to buy another property. The problem with refinancing is you are probably not able to borrow all the equity in the unit and you may end up leveraging more than you want to handle.

3. HOLD: If your unit is not performing well due to market volatility, or if you were to refinance or sell your property with the knowledge that you will be taxed or penalized with high stamp duties, it is best to hold on to your property until conditions improve.

Repeat – After you have considered all the six steps to buying property, and you have activated the equity of your investments, the next step is to repeat the process by going back to Step 1: Research.

The Six Steps to Buying Property

As you start accumulating more and more property, you need to consider more carefully your borrowing power and whether you can keep the process rolling.

Chapter Sixteen
Looking Forward

For many people a home is the largest purchase they will ever make in their lifetime, but it need not be the most difficult. These steps do not require giant leaps. If you have time and patience you can slowly grow that nest egg into a nice swanky home. Remember Monopoly©? I did not start out pushing for the biggest place I could possibly afford with all of my active income I was making, I purchased something small and set the wheels in motion and then looked for another one and continued the process until I had a few more rolling along smoothly. Eventually after some time I traded them in for bigger ones.

I am still not completely done with building my property portfolio and I am still always on the look out for more opportunities.

Currently due to all the changes in the Hong Kong stamp duties, I have decided to hold on to my units in Hong

Kong and just have them slowly grow in equity. I still enjoy watching the market change and I reached a point in my life that I decided to leave the teaching field to become a real estate advisor in Hong Kong. It still excites me when I find opportunities in the property market for my buyers.

Where do I start?

It all starts with you getting on that first rung of the ladder. If you still haven't bought any property in Hong Kong and have permanent residency, there is never a better time than now to get started.

In this book, I have told you all the sludge I have waded through to get to where I am now. It wasn't too difficult but it was definitely not easy. That is why I am trying to tell you here that the only thing you need is to be ready.

Surround yourself with the people who can help you. Never be an island floating out on your own. Right from the beginning I had people who helped me with the house hunting, the purchasing, the lending and the legal paperwork. Every step takes time and energy but there will always be people who have walked that path who can lead the way. I still work with the same buyer's agents, mortgage brokers, solicitors and bankers because it is always best to work with someone you know and trust so you make each other's lives easier.

This real estate market is continuously evolving. That is why you need someone who has his or her eyes and ears down on the ground listening and watching for the next opportunity to pop up.

Looking back, I can see that some of those decisions I made were pretty quick and for some, were a bit impulsive. However, none of my decisions were made irrationally. I was quick, decisive and most of all, I was ready when the opportunity struck. I didn't have to wait for an unnatural catastrophe to happen in order to take a swing of the bat. I decided to get into the market because I knew I was ready.

Hindsight is great to have because you can always see what you have achieved. If you have walked that path well, you can quite possibly be able to predict the direction you will be heading towards. I have talked to many people who have sought my advice and I tell them the number one destroyer of wealth is something that everybody has the ability to control – procrastination. There's no time like the present.

(On my listings page, check out the latest available listings on sale at http://michelle-cheng.com)

Where can you find Michelle Cheng?

I hope you enjoyed reading my book and I hope it sheds some light onto your thoughts about property.

Regardless of whether you are thinking about selling your property or buying a property in the short or medium term, or are just curious to receive a no-obligation valuation or advice, feel free to contact me and I will be more than happy to arrange an individual consultation with you.

Feel confident that you will be working with someone very knowledgeable and efficient in this industry.

Warmest Regards

Michelle Cheng
852 6409 8585
ms.michelle.cheng@gmail.com

www.michelle-cheng.com

Made in the USA
Columbia, SC
04 July 2017